THE POCK

BUSINE

THE POCKET BUSINESS COMMUNICATOR

A complete A–Z of ready-made business letters and documents

SHIRLEY TAYLOR

FINANCIAL TIMES
PRENTICE HALL

PEARSON EDUCATION LIMITED
Head Office:
Edinburgh Gate
Harlow CM20 2JE
Tel: +44 (0)1279 623623
Fax: +44 (0)1279 431059

London Office:
128 Long Acre, London WC2E 9AN
Tel: +44 (0)171 447 2000
Fax: +44 (0)171 240 5771

First published in Great Britain 1999

ISBN 0 273 64417 3

British Library Cataloguing in Publication Data
A CIP catalogue record for this book can be obtained from the British Library.

10 9 8 7 6 5 4 3 2 1

Typeset by Pantek Arts, Maidstone, Kent
Printed and bound by Bell & Bain Ltd, Glasgow

The Publishers' policy is to use paper manufactured from sustainable forests.

About the Author

Shirley Taylor worked as Private Secretary at director level for nine years. She has many advanced secretarial qualifications including the LCCIEB Private Secretary's Diploma (Fourth Level) and a shorthand speed of 170 wpm.

After obtaining teaching diplomas and the Certificate in Education, Shirley taught on business and secretarial courses both in the UK and overseas. She spent several years in Singapore as Training Consultant and Lecturer and was Head of Secretarial Department at a college in Bahrain, Arabian Gulf. She has also lived in Toronto, Canada.

In recent years Shirley has put her considerable experience into writing. In 1991 her first book *Communication for Business* was published by Longman – this popular textbook is now in its third edition. Since then Shirley has written *The Secretary in Training* (Textbook and Answerbook), *Practical Audio Transcription* (Workbook and Cassette) and *Gartside's Model Business Letters and Other Business Documents*.

Having lived and worked in Singapore, Bahrain and Canada as well as her native UK, Shirley now enjoys travelling to undertake consultancy projects and to conduct workshops for teachers and students and seminars on Effective Business Writing. In addition to her writing and consultancy work, Shirley is an examiner in secretarial skills for a major examining board.

You can contact Shirley on email at SAT001@aol.com

Contents

Preface

The Pocket Business Communicator is a comprehensive, one-of-a-kind reference book full of specimen documents, useful techniques and practical guidelines – all contained in a unique A-Z format.

The Pocket Business Communicator provides you with answers to all your questions about compiling business documents. This handy reference book shows you how to say what you want to say – accurately, briefly and clearly – and get the results you want. Guidance is also included on how to display documents attractively, structure your message logically and use modern business language.

With all this in an A–Z format, it means that whatever you are looking for it will be easy to find, such as articles, circulars, e-mails, faxes, goodwill letters, itineraries, leaflets, memos, minutes, notices, press releases, questionnaires, references, reports, sales letters, testimonials, unwelcome news, voluntary offers and warnings.

Some of the examples can be lifted straight from the page, or you may adapt them for your own use. The accompanying floppy disk contains all the sample documents so that it will be even easier for you to adapt the documents to meet your specific needs.

Whether you are a managing director, executive, salesman, supervisor, secretary or student, this handy reference book will help you to develop and improve your writing skills.

Don't forget to visit *The Pocket Business Communicator*'s website on www.pocketdocuments.com. On the website you will find copies of all the documents as well as lots more interesting information – a recommended further reading list, links to other interesting sites, more information about the author and a feedback form for you to let us know what you think.

Shirley Taylor

Please note: For reasons of consistency and simplicity and to avoid confusion, we have used the UK -ise spelling convention throughout this book. Readers should also be familiar with the -ize convention which many countries worldwide prefer to adopt.

Acknowledgements

I am very grateful to the following organisations for their interest and help in providing permission to reproduce copyright material:

Doctor Patient Partnership
Waterlow Business Supplies

The Pocket Business Communicator evolved from a simple discussion in Singapore with my good friend, Leslie Lim, who suggested the need for a portable, compact but comprehensive book of business documents. For your help and friendship over the last few years, Leslie, this one is for you.

A

■ ABC of good business writing

Here is your ABC checklist for composing effective business documents:

Accuracy	Check all the facts carefully Include all the relevant details Plan carefully Proofread thoroughly
Brevity	Keep sentences short Start a new paragraph every 3–5 lines Use simple expressions and simple words Use non-technical language
Clarity	Use plain, simple English Avoid formality or familiarity Write in an easy, natural style as if you are having a conversation

■ Acknowledgement

Acknowledgement letters should be sent out of courtesy when detailed replies are not called for. Acknowledgements should be sent when important documents and cheques have been received. Acknowledgements should be sent when you cannot immediately send a full reply, perhaps when a key person is absent or when a matter needs to be investigated.

Acknowledgement promising fuller reply

1 Thank you for your letter of 2 June regarding your experience when you visited our Bedford store last month.

2 I am looking into this situation and shall contact you again when I have received the results of my investigation.

1 Thank … give the background
2 Action being taken

Acknowledgement of a first order

Dear

1 I was very pleased to receive your order of 18 June for cotton prints, and welcome you as one of our customers.

2 I confirm supply of the prints at the prices stated in your letter. Delivery should be made by our own vehicles early next week. I feel confident that you will be completely satisfied with these goods and that you will find them exceptionally good value for money.

3 As you may not be aware of the wide range of goods we have available, I am enclosing a copy of our catalogue.

4 I hope that our handling of your first order with us will lead to further business between us and mark the beginning of a happy working relationship.

Yours sincerely

1 Thank you
2 Confirm prices and delivery information. Give assurance of satisfaction
3 Mention other goods and enclose catalogue
4 Close with a wish for future business dealings

Acknowledgement pointing out delayed delivery

Dear

1 Thank you for your order of 20 January.

2 Unfortunately we are presently out of stock of the model you ordered. This is due to the prolonged cold weather which has increased demand considerably. The manufacturers have, however, promised us a further supply by the end of this month. If you could wait until then we would fulfil your order promptly.

3 I am sorry we cannot meet your present order immediately, but hope to hear from you soon that delivery at the beginning of next month will be convenient for you.

Yours sincerely

1 Thank you
2 Express regret and explain
3 Ask for confirmation

■ Advertisement

Special techniques must be used for compiling advertisements:

A The advertisement must first of all attract the reader's ATTENTION
I Get the reader's INTEREST by mentioning something which will appeal to them
D Arouse the reader's DESIRE to buy or to find out more or to contact the writer
A Make the audience want to take ACTION as a result of reading the advertisement

Advertisement including reply section

1 ATTENTION: Use a catchy headline
2 INTEREST: An illustration shows an immediate appeal. Interesting information is highlighted to stand out.
3 DESIRE: Bullet points list features to arouse readers' interest
4 ACTION: Tear-off slip makes it easy to take action

Job advertisement

[1] GLOBAL

[2] Together We Excel

[3] QUALITY ENGINEER

[4] Here's your chance to join a dynamic and rapidly expanding global company. Global Communications is a global leader in the world of telecommunications. We are looking for dynamic, self-motivated team players to join us.

Responsibilities

- Ensure Global's major accounts continue to benefit from customer service and support.
- Support major accounts on technical and quality issues.
- Organise pre-sales initiatives on new products. [5]

Pre-requisites [6]

- Experience in telecommunications industry.
- ISO 9000 knowledge.
- Good people skills.

[7] We offer a 5-day week and attractive compensation package commensurate with experience and qualifications.

[8] Please send a handwritten application letter with full resumé and a recent photograph to:

Mr William Wright
Human Relations Manager
[9] Global Communications plc
14 Western Avenue
Highbury
Sheffield S26 2ES

[10] Closing date for applications: 12 July 2000

1 Logo of company
2 Headline attracts attention
3 Job title
4 Information about the company
5 Use bullet points
6 State what you want from applicants
7 Emphasise compensation package
8 State if applications are to be handwritten
9 Name/title/company name and address
10 Closing date for applications

■ Agenda

Sometimes a memo is written giving a list of agenda items to be discussed at a meeting (see MEMO). More often than not the notice and agenda are prepared as a separate document.

Notice = The portion at the top giving details of the type, place, day, date and time of the meeting.

Agenda = A list of topics to be discussed at the meeting.

Notice and Agenda for Operations Meeting

[1] GLOBAL COMMUNICATIONS
OPERATIONS MEETING

[2] The next Operations Meeting will be held in the Conference Room at 1030 on Monday 14 March 200-.

AGENDA

1 Apologies for absence
[3] 2 Minutes of last meeting
3 Matters arising
    3.1 Training courses (Martin Holbrook)
[4]
    3.2 Annual dinner and dance (Betty Roberts)
4 Visit to Middle East (Terry Williams)
[5] 5 New branch in Ontario, Canada
6 10th Anniversary Celebrations (Ben Hunter)
7 Any other business
[6]
8 Date of next meeting

1 Company name and meeting
2 Notice: type, place, time, day and date
3 First 3 items are Ordinary Business
4 Enumerate when an item has more than one point
5 Special Business
6 Final 2 items of Ordinary Business

■ Apology

When it is necessary to apologise for something, you must ensure that you get the tone right. A complaint requiring an apology is a unique opportunity to build good will.

Apology for poor service

Dear Mrs Richardson

[1] Thank you for your letter of 3 March pointing out the poor service you received when you visited our store in Newton Road recently.

[2] The incident you describe was most unlike the usual high standards of service and courtesy which we try to inculcate in all our staff. The member of staff concerned has been reprimanded and has expressed his regret.

[3] I am pleased to enclose a gift voucher for £25 which may be used in any Orian store. If I can be of any further help to you please do not hesitate to let me know.

Yours sincerely

1 Thank … brief summary
2 Indicate commitment to quality; state action taken as a result of complaint
3 Send gift voucher by way of compensation; finish with good wishes

Apology to competitor to avoid possible legal action for libel

Dear Mr Smart

[1] WITHOUT PREJUDICE

[2] Thank you for your letter of 14 July pointing out the implications of our advertisement in this month's *Car World* 'Be a winner with Westlake'.

[3] We would like to express our apologies for any implications damaging to your interests. Such implications were quite unintentional and only seen through hindsight. The offending advertisement has been withdrawn.

[4] We would be prepared to send an explanatory letter to *Car World* for printing in their next issue as you request. However we feel that this action would bring to the attention of readers an issue which they may not have been aware of, so we feel such action would not benefit either of our companies.

Yours sincerely

1 Without prejudice used as heading
2 Thank … brief summary
3 Apologise … action taken
4 Conclusion

■ Application (see EMPLOYMENT APPLICATION)

■ Appointment

Cancellation of appointment

Dear Mr Newman

1 2 I am so sorry that I had to cancel our meeting yesterday at such short notice. As my secretary explained to you an urgent matter came up and I had to deal with it immediately.

3 I understand that our appointment has been rearranged for next Thursday 17 August at 10.30 am. I shall look forward to seeing you then.

Yours sincerely

1 Apologise
2 State reason for cancellation
3 State date/time of new appointment; finish with good wishes

■ Appointment letter (see also REJECTION OF APPLICATION)

Letters of appointment are in essence quite formal.

Letter offering employment

Dear Mr Johnson

1 Thank you for attending the interview yesterday. I am pleased to offer you the post of General Manager of our Leeds branch commencing on 1 December 200-.

2 Your duties will be as outlined at the interview and as described on the attached Job Description.

3 This appointment carries a commencing salary of £25,000 per annum which will be reviewed annually. Other terms and conditions of employment are stated on the attached Contract of Employment.

4 Please confirm your acceptance of this offer and that you will be able to commence work on 1 December.

Yours sincerely

1 Refer to interview; offer post – give title and commencement date
2 Refer to Job Description
3 State salary and other terms and conditions of employment
4 Ask for confirmation

■ Article (see also PRESS RELEASE and NEWSLETTER)

When writing an article to appear in a magazine or house journal remember to write as if the magazine is speaking, ie third person, reported speech. Follow the guidelines shown in this example.

[1] SUPERSTARS TEAM GAIN SECOND PLACE

[2] The stamina and strength of 3 Global employees were put to the test when they competed in the European finals of the Tech-stars competition held in Rotterdam, Holland.

[3] Global Holdings was invited to the European finals after winning the regional heat at Leeds and being runners-up in the British final.

[4] All entrants must work with information technology in some way, and Global has entered a team every year since 1985 when they won the European final. This year's competition consisted of 8 strenuous, athletic-based events in one day, in which 3 of the 5 team members had to compete.

[5] Unfortunately, due to holiday commitments this year's Global team entered without two of their top athletes, leaving John Holmes, Martin Wilson and Andrew Johnson to compete in this event. After a long day's hard work the team then had to face the final event which was a 2000 metre steeplechase, and all team members performed extremely well in this.

[6] The final result was that Global put in a very creditable performance and achieved second place. Well done to the team!

1 Catchy headline
2 Give main message quickly in first paragraph
3 Use short self-contained paragraphs
4 Use double spacing in case of editing
5 Make it a human-interest story
6 Finish with a snappy conclusion

■ Business letter layout

The fully-blocked layout, using open punctuation, is the most popular layout for all business documents. It is quick and easy to prepare with a businesslike appearance.

Apollo Communications

14 Western Avenue, Highbury, Sheffield S26 2ES
1 *Telephone: +44 114 2823432 Fax: +44 114 2887234*
Email: Apollo@A-Z.com.uk

2 ST/KL

25 June 200_

Mrs Irith Williams
3 Williams Publishing Co Ltd
28 Hunter Avenue
London
WC1 8TJ

4 Dear Irith

5 FULLY BLOCKED LETTER LAYOUT

This layout has become firmly established as the most popular way of setting out letters, fax messages, memos, reports – in fact all business communications. The main feature of fully blocked style is that all lines begin at the left-hand margin.

6 Open punctuation is usually used with the fully-blocked layout. This means that no punctuation marks are necessary in the reference, date, inside address, salutation and closing section. Of course essential punctuation must still be used in the text of the message itself. However remember to use commas minimally today, they should only be used when their omission would make the sense of the message unclear.

Consistency is important in layout and spacing of all documents. It is usual to leave just one clear line space between each section.

I enclose some other examples of fully blocked layout as used in fax messages and memoranda.

Most people agree that this layout is very attractive, easy to produce as well as businesslike.

7 Yours sincerely

8 SHIRLEY TAYLOR
9 Secretarial Consultant

10 Encs

11 Copy: Pradeep Jethi, Publisher
Amelia Lakin, Publishing Co-ordinator

Notes overleaf.

1 Letterheaded paper
2 Reference (initials of writer/typist) and date (day, month, year)
3 Inside address
4 Salutation
5 Heading
6 Body of letter (one line space between paragraphs)
7 Complimentary close
8 Name of sender
9 Sender's designation or department
10 Enc (if anything is enclosed)
11 If more than one copy is circulated, use alphabetical order

C

■ Chasing letter (see COLLECTION LETTER)

■ Checklist

Checklists are often used when describing a procedure to be followed. Bullet points or numbered points may be used. As in this example, be consistent with the wording of each point. Using verbs as the first word is a good idea as it ensures grammatical parallelism.

Checklist

1 SUCCESS IN BUSINESS – SOME BASIC RULES

2 1 Measure your success in business by your results. At the end of the day, results count, not time or effort.

3 2 Write down your ideas as soon as you have them, otherwise you may forget.

3 Work out a solution to a problem before you discuss it with your superior.

4 Assume that no-one can keep a secret.

4 5 Schedule and prioritise your work to fit in with your personal peaks.

6 Do not patronise. Treat everyone with equal respect and dignity.

7 Do not let stress show in front of clients, colleagues or employers. A deep breath will help.

8 Acknowledge contributions from others.

5 9 Take advantage of winning streaks.

6 10 Be true to yourself, as well as your career and your interests.

11 Know your key skills and abilities, and use them whenever possible.

12 Finish stronger than you start.

1 Headings
2 Continue second line at the start of first, rather than under the numbers
3 Use verbs for the start of each point
4 Keep points short and self-contained
5 Check consistent use of verbs as first word
6 Align numbers correctly

■ Circular letter (see also SALES LETTER, SURVEY LETTER)

Circular letters should be made as personal as possible. Even though they will be sent to many people, remember that they will be read by only one person at a time.

1 Dear Customer

2 EVERYTHING GOES IN SPRING SALE

3 Circle Saturday 2 April on your calendar! That is when our fantastic jewellery sale begins. You will want to be at our store at 9 am when the doors open.

Gold, silver, necklaces, earrings, bracelets - absolutely everything will be reduced by 10 to 50 per cent. Take a look at these fantastic reductions:

4 Gold link earrings - originally £60 now £30
Matching bracelet - originally £90 now £50
Necklaces (gold and silver) – from as little as £20
Earrings (gold and silver) – from only £5

5 You will not want to miss our spectacular one-week only sale. So be here bright and early on Saturday 2 April. The early bird will catch the biggest savings.

6 See you at the sale you will not want to miss!

Yours sincerely

1 Use singular expressions ('Customer' not 'Customers')
2 Give the gist in the heading
3 Word the first paragraphs so the reader wants to know more
4 Give examples
5 Use individual expressions in the body of the letter, 'you' NOT 'all of you' or 'you all'
6 Keep it friendly and informal

■ Collection letter

The style and tone of a collection letter will depend on the age of the debt, whether the customer is usually late in payment, and other factors. Use restraint when writing collection letters. Be polite and businesslike.

C

A first collection letter

> Dear
>
> [1] ACCOUNT NUMBER 2348XJ
>
> [2] As you are usually very prompt in settling your accounts, we are surprised that we have not received payment of your September account which is well over a month overdue.
>
> [3] In case you have not received our statement of account sent on 2 October, a copy is enclosed. [4] You will note that this shows a balance owing of £1500.58 and we hope this will receive your early attention.
>
> Yours sincerely

1 Account number
2 Express surprise
3 Give details
4 State balance and request action

Second collection letter

> Dear
>
> [1] ACCOUNT NUMBER 2348XJ
>
> [2] We note that a reply has not yet been received to our letter of 5 November requesting settlement of this account.
>
> [3] The amount still owing on this account is £1500.58 and we hope to receive this soon together with an explanation about the late payment.
>
> Yours sincerely

1 Account number
2 Refer to previous letter
3 State amount owing and request action

Third collection letter

Dear

1 ACCOUNT NUMBER 2348XJ

2 We have not received replies to our two previous requests dated 5 and 16 November in connection with £1500.58 still owing on this account.

3 It is with regret that we have reached the stage when we must ask you for immediate payment. Unless payment is received by 18 December we will have no choice but to take further action.

4 We sincerely hope that this will not be necessary.

Yours sincerely

1 Account number
2 Refer to previous letters; state amount owing
3 Express regret; give deadline for payment
4 Courteous close

Final collection letter

Dear

1 ACCOUNT NUMBER 2348XJ

2 We very much regret that we have received no reply to our letter of 28 November. This letter referred to our previous letters dated 5 and 16 November regarding the long overdue payment on this account of £1500.58.

3 We cannot allow this amount to remain unpaid indefinitely. Unless the amount due is paid or a satisfactory explanation received by the end of this month, we shall be reluctantly compelled to put this matter in the hands of our solicitors.

Yours sincerely

1 Account number
2 Refer to previous letters and amount owing
3 State your position and give ultimatum

■ Complaint

There are bound to be occasions when it is necessary to deal with complaints, no matter how good our intentions and efforts. Complaints may be necessary due to incorrect goods, unsatisfactory goods, poor service, late delivery, etc. Always write promptly so that your position is strong.

C

Complaint about faulty goods

Dear

1 We recently received 50 Flip Flop Frogs in accordance with our order 453FT dated 16 June.

2 Unfortunately these Frogs don't flip so they are just a complete flop. The Flip Flop Frogs appear to have faulty mechanisms which caused them to fall over instead of flipping over as promised in your catalogue.

3 I hope you can deliver a further fully functional 50 Flip Flop Frogs urgently. These faulty ones will be returned with your driver when delivery is made.

4 Your products have always been of good quality and have sold well in my store in the past. Therefore this is a great disappointment to us. I hope to hear from you soon on this matter.

Yours sincerely

1 Introduction and background information
2 Give full details of complaint
3 Action expected
4 Courteous close

Reply to complaint about faulty goods

Dear

1 Thank you for your letter of 18 March. I was very sorry to hear about the problems you experienced with the mechanisms of our Flip Flop Frogs.

2 Since your order was despatched we found out that this particular batch of Flip Flop Frogs was faulty. There was a fault on one of the machines in our factory which caused this malfunction.

3 This problem has now been rectified and we have today sent a further 50 Flip Flop Frogs to you. Our driver has been instructed to collect the 50 faulty Frogs from you. Please ensure that the box is clearly marked 'FAULTY'.

4 Once again our apologies for the inconvenience you have been caused. I am sure you will find that these Flip Flop Frogs sell well as they have proved to be very popular.

Yours sincerely

1 Thank … express regret
2 Reply to complaint
3 Action taken
4 Apologise and close courteously

Complaint about poor service

Dear Sirs

1 I regret having to write to tell you how disappointed I have been regarding my purchase of new glasses from your shop.

2 I ordered my glasses on 6 October and was thrilled when I was told they had arrived less than a week later. However the lenses had not been fixed to the frames correctly, and also the bi-focal vision needed adjustment. Since then there have been several mix-ups. My first replacement pair did not have the anti-reflective coating on them. Yesterday I was informed that another replacement pair had arrived at your shop but again they were faulty.

3 I paid for my glasses in good faith in October and now almost 2 months later I have still not received the proper pair. In the circumstances I feel that I should be given a substantial refund for all the inconvenience that I have been caused.

4 I must stress that I still expect to receive the correct glasses. I shall be most disappointed if this matter does not reach a satisfactory conclusion very soon.

Yours faithfully

1 Introduction
2 Give details of complaint in correct order
3 Conclusion … state action expected
4 Firm closing paragraph

Reply from supplier

Dear Mrs Turner

1 Thank you for your letter of 14 December.

2 On behalf of Eyes Right I would like to apologise most sincerely for the problems you have experienced in receiving your new glasses. This is most unlike the speedy, professional service which we pride ourselves on.

3 As a gesture of goodwill I would like to offer you a refund of £100 to cover your travelling costs and inconvenience which you have incurred. Our cheque is enclosed.

4 I understand from the manufacturers that your glasses should be arriving in our store during the next few days. I will give you a call as soon as they are with us to arrange an appointment for you to come down to collect them.

5 Many apologies again for the problems you have experienced.

Yours sincerely

1 Refer to letter
2 Apologise
3 Make offer for inconvenience … enclose cheque
4 State further details
5 Apologise again

Complaint about poor quality of purchase

Dear Mr Long

[1] I feel quite sick as I write this letter. I have just prepared my dinner this evening, which comprised mainly items which I bought at Omega Supermarket this morning.

[2] One item which I put on my plate was some of Omega's own brand Coleslaw. I wonder if you can imagine my horror when I found what looks like a horrible piece of gristle in the portion of coleslaw which I put on my plate. Thank goodness I did not put this in my mouth because I am a vegetarian, and as such I am most careful to choose only items which are marked as suitable for vegetarians. To find this disgusting animal part in my coleslaw has caused me severe distress and upset.

[3] I have thrown the coleslaw in the bin and am enclosing the lid for your reference together with the offending gristle.

[4] As a regular visitor to Omega Supermarket I expected your company to have very strict health and safety guidelines in force. My experience with this coleslaw has shown that the procedures in place leave a lot to be desired and I hope you will instigate an immediate review of policy and procedures.

Yours sincerely

1 Introduction
2 Give details in logical order
3 Action taken
4 Firm close and request for investigation

■ Condolence

Letters of condolence are not easy to write. There can be no set pattern to such letters since a lot depends on your relationship with the recipient. Keep your letter short but say what you feel warmly and sincerely. The aim is to offer comfort and support to the bereaved person. Condolence letters are much better if handwritten.

Letter of condolence after long illness

Dear Mary

1 I felt I must write to say how very sorry I was to hear the sad news. Even though John has been in hospital for some time and it was known that he was not likely to recover, this is still a very hard time for you. If there is any consolation now it is that he is finally at peace.

2 Please accept our sincere condolences and deepest sympathy. Our thoughts are with you.

Yours

1 Tone is important in a letter of condolence
2 Offer condolences

Letter of condolence to a friend

Dear Ellen

1 I was devastated when I heard the news today about Martin's passing.

2 Martin was a very dear friend, well-loved by his many friends and family. His cheerful outlook, his genuine warmth and his generous nature will be missed desperately. Most of all I will miss his unique sense of humour and fun.

3 I have valued your friendship and Martin's over the last 15 years. At this very sad time I send you my love and assurance of support and continued friendship.

4 I will be in touch again very soon. Meanwhile if you need any help at all just let me know.

Yours

1 Introduction
2 Express personal feelings
3 Give support
4 Offer help

■ Confirmation

A letter of confirmation is very simple. Just mention that you are confirming whatever it is and then spell out the details.

Confirmation of job offer

Dear Mr Wilson

1 Thank you for your letter of 12 June offering me the post of Financial Controller.

2 I confirm my acceptance of this post and will be free to start work on 1 August 200-.

3 I look forward to joining your company.

Yours sincerely

1 Refer to letter of offer
2 Confirm acceptance … state start date
3 Close

Confirmation of meeting

Dear Peter

1 Thank you for lunch yesterday and for showing me around your new offices. Your new facilities are certainly most impressive.

2 I am pleased to confirm that Global Training would like you to produce a 15 minute video to mark the occasion of our 10th year of business. It is planned to show the video at our 10th Anniversary Celebration which will be held at the Regal Prince Hotel in July.

3 I look forward to seeing you again at our head office at 1030 on Wednesday 14 March along with our Communications Director, Philip Drew. We are both looking forward to seeing your presentation of ideas for this special video.

4 If you need any further details before we meet please give me a call.

Yours sincerely

1 Refer to meeting
2 Confirm relevant details
3 State further meeting – time/day/date – and reason
4 Close

Confirmation of telephone call

> Dear Shirley
>
> 1 Further to our telephone conversation this morning I confirm that we are interested in your suggestion for a book entitled *Pocket Business Communicator – A Complete A–Z of Ready-made Business Documents*.
>
> 2 Please put together a formal proposal for this project outlining the concept, target audience, main features and draft list of contents.
>
> 3 As soon as we receive your proposal I will be able to undertake some market research and obtain the necessary feedback so that we can take this proposal further.
>
> 4 I look forward to hearing from you soon.
>
> Yours sincerely

1 Refer to call; give background details.
2 State further details needed.
3 Follow-up details
4 Close

C

■ Congratulations

Letters of congratulation are a good way of promoting goodwill. They are written on the occasion of a promotion, marriage, birth, success in an examination or a special honour.

Congratulations on a promotion

> Dear Henry
>
> 1 Many congratulations on your recent appointment to the Board of Global Chemicals plc.
>
> 2 I am delighted that the many years of service you have given to your company have been rewarded in this way.
>
> 3 My fellow directors join me in sending you our very best wishes for the future.
>
> Yours sincerely

1 Specific congratulations
2 Add some personal comments
3 Close with best wishes

Congratulations to a work colleague on a birth

Dear Martin

1 I have just heard from your secretary that you have become the proud father of twins. Many congratulations to you and your wife.

2 I am sure you will have lots of sleepless nights over the next few months, but no doubt you will be amply rewarded by a great deal of joy which your children will bring you in the years to come.

3 Please pass on my very best wishes and congratulations to Helen.

Yours sincerely

1 Specific congratulations
2 Add some personal comments
3 Close with best wishes

Congratulations on a public honour

Dear Dr Anson

1 I was delighted to see your name in the New Year's Honours List today. I would like to add my congratulations to the many you will be receiving at this exciting time.

2 The many people who know you and your work will be as pleased as I am to hear of this well-earned award. It is good to know that your outstanding work has been so suitably rewarded.

3 With very best wishes

Yours sincerely

1 Specific congratulations
2 Personal comments
3 Close

■ Continuation sheet

When a letter, memo or fax message has to be continued on a second or subsequent page, always head the second or subsequent pages with the following details – just in case the first page is somehow separated from the rest.

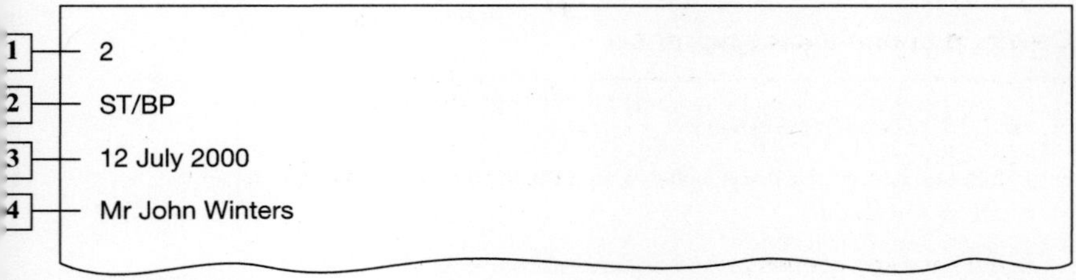

1 Page number
2 Reference
3 Date
4 Addressee's name

When using a continuation sheet, remember these guidelines:

- It is not necessary to put 'continued', or 'cont' or '2/....' at the foot of the first page.
- Always take over at least 3 or 4 lines of text to a second or subsequent page.
- Try to start a new page with a new paragraph - this looks much better.

■ Covering letter (see also APPLICATION)

If you have an estimate, order, quotation, specification or other document to send to someone you may wish to compose a covering letter. A covering memo is also used to enclose a report or other document. Such letters or memos should only be very simple but you may have to explain something about the accompanying document(s) or material.

Covering memo enclosing report

1 REPORT ON STAFF CANTEEN

2 I have completed my investigations into the staff canteen as you requested. My report is enclosed.

3 If you have any queries please do not hesitate to let me know.

4 Enc

1 Heading
2 Enclose the report
3 Close
4 Don't forget Enc

Covering letter enclosing quotation

Dear Mr Robinson

1 Thank you for your enquiry of 20 February. I am pleased to enclose our quotation as requested. All these items can be delivered from stock.

2 Our current catalogue is also enclosed in which you will find details of our full range of office furniture and accessories.

3 If you have any queries regarding our quotation please do not hesitate to give me a call.

Yours sincerely

1 Refer to enquiry … enclose quotation
2 Enclose catalogue
3 Close

■ Curriculum vitae (see RESUMÉ)

■ Death of colleague

When a colleague dies it may be necessary to write to employees or customers. Such a letter should be brief but written with feeling.

Death of colleague

> Dear
>
> 1 It is with much sadness that I have to tell you of the death of our Finance Manager, Keith Johnson. Keith was ill in hospital for a several weeks before he passed away peacefully in his sleep.
>
> 2 During his 12 years with the company, Keith made an enormous contribution to the development of the business. His hard work, good humour and his compassion were greatly appreciated by all his colleagues and associates.
>
> 3 For the time being please contact Martin Tyson, Financial Controller, regarding any matters you would usually raise with Keith.
>
> Yours sincerely

1. Express sadness … announce death
2. Mention contribution to company … personal qualities
3. State who to contact in future

■ Deferred payment

There may occasionally be circumstances which mean you are unable to meet all your month-end commitments. It is much better to write a letter than to be chased in a few weeks' time. The aim of your letter will be to assure your creditors and to secure their agreement without worrying them unduly.

Letter requesting more time to pay

Dear Mrs Coleman

1 INVOICE NUMBER 432TM

2 This invoice dated 23 September in the sum of £5,560.00 is due for payment at the end of this month. I would like to request a slightly extended period in which to complete this payment.

3 Unfortunately we have had a large fire in our factory and this destroyed a lot of our stocks. Our claim is now with our insurers and we are awaiting settlement. Meanwhile we are in an embarrassing financial situation. Production has now resumed but obviously we have a lot of outstanding orders which we must fulfil. This is having an adverse effect on our cash flow.

4 I hope you will agree to our deferring payment of this account until 31 December. Thereafter we hope that conditions will have improved so that we can revert to normal terms of trading.

5 As you know our accounts have always been settled promptly in the past. It is with regret now that I am forced to make this request. I thank you for your understanding.

Yours sincerely

1 Invoice number
2 State invoice date and amount … request extension
3 Explain circumstances surrounding request for extension
4 Give date for deferring payment
5 Express regret and thanks

■ Dismissal (see also REPRIMAND and WARNING LETTER)

The dismissal of an employee can only be undertaken on well-defined grounds. This must normally be preceded by at least one warning. Grounds for dismissal must be specific, measured if possible against the company's terms and conditions of employment (such as working hours) or against the employee's job description or specification. Dismissal arises basically due to the employee breaking his or her contract of employment with the company. The employee should understand and if possible accept the reason(s) for dismissal, otherwise he/she could seek compensation for unfair dismissal. If the employee belongs to a trade union you should contact the local union representative and explain the circumstances before taking any action.

The length of notice served on an employee will depend on his/her legal rights and on the contract of employment – this may be a week, a month or longer. For long-serving employees there is a legal minimum period of notice. You should be familiar with the formal requirements.

When an employee commits a gross offence such as theft or vandalism, he or she may be subject to a summary dismissal.

Letter giving an employee a month's notice

1 Dear John

Further to our discussion, I confirm that you have agreed to leave the company
2 with effect from one month from now, ie on Friday 29 August.

This action follows my warning letters to you dated 25 June and 8 July and further instances of your breaching company rules - smoking in prohibited areas and rudeness to customers. All these incidents have been discussed with you
3 and officially reported under the company's general conditions of employment.

If you find another position before the end of the month we will be happy to release you.

Yours sincerely

1 Refer to discussion; confirm leaving date
2 Refer to warning letters and give details.
3 State early release possible

Summary dismissal

> Dear Mr Winton
>
> [1] I confirm that you are dismissed from the company with immediate effect. This action follows the discovery that you were caught stealing money from a colleague's handbag today, 25 July. [2] You were also sent warning letters regarding unsatisfactory conduct dated 29 April and 15 June.
>
> [3] Our cheque for one week's salary in lieu of notice is enclosed.
>
> Yours sincerely

1 Confirm immediate dismissal. State reason why
2 Refer to previous warnings
3 Enclose any salary due

■ Donation appeal (see also CIRCULAR LETTER, SALES LETTER)

A letter requesting donations needs to be written to appeal to the emotions and sympathy of the reader. Such letters are usually sent out with a leaflet explaining more about the cause concerned and a form for recipients to return with a donation.

Letter appealing for sympathy

> Dear Reader
>
> [1] You can walk around your home, at work, in the streets, in the country. You take this ability for granted, yet the simple act of walking around is something which is denied to thousands of people all over the world - those who are born crippled, or those who are crippled by accident or illness.
>
> [2] It is estimated that every 5 minutes in Britain a deformed child is born or a child is crippled by accident or illness. This means that every day there could be almost 300 more crippled children than there were yesterday.
>
> [3] This probably strikes you as incredibly unfair. Much of what is unfair in life is something which we can do little about. However here is one very important inequality which we can all help with. The enclosed leaflet explains how you can help, even in a small way. While you are counting your blessings and thinking how lucky you are, please read this leaflet carefully.
>
> Yours sincerely

1 Appeal to human nature
2 Quote some facts and statistics if possible
3 Refer to leaflet and subtly request help

■ Electronic mail

Electronic mail, or e-mail as it is commonly known, has evolved as an effective, low-cost and quick method of communication with friends and colleagues all over the world. It is quick and efficient, it reduces time spent on the telephone calls, it reduces the amount of paper wasted, it even works nights and weekends. With e-mail, written communication has never been easier.

When an e-mail message is sent, it may be received within seconds when the recipient 'logs-on' to his or her e-mail system. Remember to proof-read your e-mail message carefully before clicking 'send' because once you have done this you cannot call it back for second thoughts!

E-mail messages are much less formal than letters, memos, fax messages or other communications. It is tempting to disregard proper writing procedures with e-mails, but you should really plan an e-mail message just as thoughtfully as you would a conventional message.

E-mail to a business colleague

To Amelia.Lakin@pearsoned-ema.com

From SAT001@aol.com (Shirley Taylor)

Date Monday 21 January 1999

Time 4:30:27 GMT

Subject A-Z of Business Communications

1 Hello Amelia

2 Thanks so much for your e-mail today. I'm so glad to hear that you are as excited as I am about this new project.

I've been working hard on the first draft of this new title over the last couple of months. I'm hoping to finalise everything by the end of next month.

3 I agree that it would be good to meet to discuss this further and I can show you some of my manuscript. I confirm that next Friday 29 January will be fine. I know a super place which is close to the M1 where they serve great food. Turn off the M1 at junction 30, then turn right to Barlborough and look for the De Rodes Arms – you can't miss it. I'll see you there around 12.00 noon.

4 Best wishes

Shirley

1 Informality is the rule in e-mails
2 Abbreviations and contractions are used as in speech
3 Include all necessary details but in a more chatty, conversational style
4 No formal complimentary close

■ Emoticons and other symbols

In actual conversations we use facial expressions, body language and voice inflections to convey a lot of our meaning. In e-mail messages we can use emoticons to replace such physical and verbal clues. To read these emoticons, tilt your head to the left.

:-)	Smile
;-)	Wink
:-(	Frown
:-D	Laugh
:'-(	Crying
:-[	Fed up/Disgusted
:-/	Perplexed
8-O	Amazed
:-X	My lips are sealed
<g>	grin
<bg>	big grin
<weg>	wicked evil grin

In e-mail or on the chat lines some acronyms and abbreviations may be used. These are more often used in personal e-mails rather than in business, and you must remember to use such abbreviations only when you are sure the recipient will understand them.

ASAP	As soon as possible
B4	Before
BCNU	Be seeing you
BTW	By the way
CUL	See you later
F2F	Face-to-face
FWIW	For what it's worth
FYI	For your information
GMTA	Great minds think alike
IMHO	In my humble opinion
JIC	Just in case
LOL	Laughing out loud
OIC	Oh, I see
OTOH	On the other hand
RSN	Real soon now
TIA	Thanks in advance
TPTB	The powers that be
TOL	Tons of love

■ Employment application

The aim of your application letter is to ensure you a place at the interview and as a general rule it should be kept short. Read the job advertisement carefully as it may stipulate that applications must be handwritten. It is good practice to prepare a separate curriculum vitae or resumé (see RESUMÉ) to accompany your application letter.

Application for advertised post

1 — 26 Windsor Road
CHINGFORD
CH4 6PY

15 May 200–

2 — Mrs W R Jenkinson
Personnel Manager
Leyland & Bailey Ltd
Nelson Works
CLAPTON
CH5 8HA

Dear Mrs Jenkinson

PRIVATE SECRETARY TO MANAGING DIRECTOR

3 — I was interested to see your advertisement in today's Daily Telegraph and would like to be considered for this post.

4 — I am presently working as Private Secretary to the General Manager at a manufacturing company and have a wide range of responsibilities. These include attending and taking minutes of meetings and interviews, dealing with callers and correspondence in my employer's absence, and supervising junior staff, as well as the usual secretarial duties.

5 — The kind of work in which your company is engaged particularly interests me. I would welcome the opportunity it would afford to use my language abilities which are not utilised in my present post.

6 — A copy of my curriculum vitae is enclosed with copies of testimonials from former employers.

7 — I hope to hear from you soon and to be given the opportunity to present myself at an interview.

Yours sincerely

Jean Carson

JEAN CARSON (Miss)

Encs

1 The writer's address is placed at the top right-hand corner of the letter
2 All other details begin at the left margin in fully blocked style. (It would be satisfactory to place the date at the right if preferred.)
3 Mention the post and where you saw the advertisement
4 Give an outline of your present post and briefly discuss your duties
5 An indication of why you are interested in the advertised post would be useful
6 Enclose your CV and copies of testimonials if available
7 Suitable close

Unsolicited application

An unsolicited application is one that is not asked for. When writing such a letter you should show how your qualifications and experience could be used by the company to which you are writing.

Dear Sir/Madam

[1] I have recently returned to the UK after spending 2 years teaching in Singapore, and I am presently looking for a teaching position here.

[2] Before I went to Singapore I worked as a teacher in Surrey for 5 years, after obtaining my Certificate in Education in 1993. As you will see from my enclosed Curriculum Vitae, I taught the whole range of secretarial subjects as well as word processing and information technology. I have also had experience of acting as NVQ Co-ordinator at Supreme Training College in Tring.

[3] In Singapore I gained much valuable experience teaching students on courses leading to LCCIEB Private Secretary's Diploma as well as Pitman examinations. I also helped with curriculum and materials development in the college.

[4] While looking for a full-time teaching post I am doing some temporary work. This is proving quite interesting and is giving me some valuable experience.

[5] I am very keen to find a job in the York area and hope that there is a suitable position available at your college. I will be happy to attend an interview at which my application can be discussed in more detail.

[6] I hope to hear from you soon.

Yours sincerely

1 Background information
2 Brief details of experience and qualifications, enclosing resumé
3 Further relevant details
4 Explain what you are doing now
5 State what you are hoping for
6 Close

■ Enquiry

When writing a general letter of enquiry always be specific in the details you require, eg prices, delivery details, terms of payment. When replying to an enquiry, double check to make sure that every query in the letter has been answered.

An enquiry

> Dear Sir/Madam
>
> [1] I recently visited the Ideal Home Exhibition in London and was interested to see a sample of Costello plastic tile flooring which you manufacture. I believe this type of floor covering would be suitable for the ground floor of my house. However I have not been able to find anyone in my area who is familiar with this tiling.
>
> [2] Would you please let me know in what colours and designs these tiles can be supplied, and also whether any special preparation would be necessary for the underflooring?
>
> [3] I believe it will be necessary to employ a specialist to lay the floor professionally. In this case I wonder if you are able to recommend someone in my area?
>
> [4] I hope to hear from you soon.
>
> Yours faithfully

1 Background information
2 Request information
3 Other information needed
4 Close

A reply to this enquiry

Dear Mr Marshall

1 Thank you for your letter dated 18 September enquiring about our Costello plastic tile flooring. I have pleasure in enclosing a copy of our new catalogue which shows the designs and full range of colours in which these tiles are supplied.

2 I am happy to recommend Cover-Up, 25 High Street, Bedford, as a very reliable firm who carry out all our work in your area. I have taken the liberty of asking them to contact you as soon as possible. Their consultant will be able to inspect your floors and advise you on what preparation is necessary and whether dampness is likely to cause a problem.

3 Costello plastic tile flooring is hard-wearing and if the tiles are laid professionally I am sure that the work will give you lasting satisfaction.

4 If you have any further queries please let me know, otherwise I am sure that you will be very happy with the work of Cover-Up.

Yours sincerely

1 Thank … enclose catalogue
2 Recommend local specialist and services
3 Assurance of quality
4 Close

F

■ Fax message

The fax machine revolutionised the world of communications and despite e-mail it is still one of the most popular methods of written communication today. Fax combines the immediacy of the telephone with the permanence of the written record. In particular the fax machine has replaced the airmail letter in relations with business contacts overseas. A reply can now be received within 24 hours instead of taking a couple of weeks.

Fax cover sheets

Most companies have a standard printed form or cover sheet for use when sending fax messages which extend to several pages. The cover sheet is then used to convey a simple message drawing the reader's attention to the accompanying pages.

Apollo Communications

Fax message

To:	Sarah Turner	**Fax No:**	0114 2877068
From:	Michael Newman, Sales Manager	**Date:**	25 June 2000
Copy:	Janet Grant, Personnel Manager	**Pages:**	2
Subject:	ADVERTISEMENT FOR SALES REPRESENTATIVES		

☐ **Urgent** ☐ **For Review** ☐ **Please Comment** ☐ **Please Reply** ☐ **Please Recycle**

MESSAGE

Thank you for sending the draft copy of our advertisement to be placed in The South Yorkshire Times next Monday 4 July. I have made a couple of amendments and am sending it back to you.

Please let me see the amended copy before final printing.

Apollo Communications plc
14 Western Avenue, Highbury, Sheffield S26 2ES

Telephone: +44 114 2823432 Fax: +44 114 2887234
Email: Apollo@A-Z.com.uk

F

Fax message

When preparing your own fax message, the fully-blocked style can be used. In this example note the important headings which should be included on all your fax messages:

Apollo Communications plc
14 Western Avenue, Highbury, Sheffield S26 2ES
Telephone: +44 114 2823432   Fax: +44 114 2887234
1 Email: Apollo@A–Z.com.uk

2 FAX MESSAGE

To	Alan Lim, Manager
Company	Apollo Communications (South East Asia) Pte Ltd
Fax No	+65 2345287
3 From	Helen Robinson, Manager (UK)
Ref	AL/ST
Date	14 July 2000
4 Total Pages	1

5

6 COMMUNICATIONS CONFERENCE – SINGAPORE

Our Chief Executive, Lawrence Reed, has unfortunately broken his leg while on holiday in Canada. He will be in hospital in Toronto for approximately one week and his return to the UK will be delayed until early July.

7 Mr Reed contacted me today asking if I would take his place at the Communications Conference to be held in Singapore next month.

I have arranged to fly on BA 21 on Monday 8 August arriving at Singapore Changi Airport at 1830 hours on that day. I hope you can arrange for someone to meet me at the airport. I shall need accommodation from 8–12 August, and shall return to the UK on 12 August on the 2315 flight.

Please fax to me the full programme details for this conference.

8 I look forward to meeting you.

9 Copy: Lawrence Reed's Secretary - for information

1 Letterheaded paper
2 Include this main heading
3 All these details are essential; align them neatly
4 State the number of pages being sent
5 A salutation may be used if preferred
6 Subject heading
7 The body of the message is composed just like a letter
8 A complimentary close and signature section are not necessary
9 Indicate any copies

■ Follow-up letter

A follow-up letter may be sent if you have not received a reply to your first letter. A follow-up may also be sent to provide information which was not previously available. A follow-up after a special sale or event is also a good idea as it reinforces positive contact and encourages repeat business.

Follow-up sales letter

Dear Mr Kelly

1 I wrote to you on 15 October describing our new Gro-More range and enclosing our latest catalogue. I have not received a reply from you and wonder if you actually received my letter?

2 I will be very happy to answer any questions you may have about our Gro-More range and explain the unique features and benefits to you. Alternatively I would be pleased to arrange for one of our representatives to visit you and bring some samples to show you.

3 Your custom is very valuable to us and if there is any way I can help you please do not hesitate to call me.

Yours sincerely

1 Refer to letter and details
2 Suggest call from representative
3 Courteous close

F

Follow-up after a function

Dear Mandy

1 It was a pleasure to have your company's Annual Dinner and Dance at our hotel last week. I enjoyed working with you and hope that you feel the function was a success.

2 If there is anything that I can do to help you in the future, please do not hesitate to give me a call.

Yours sincerely

1 Refer to function
2 Close

Follow-up to close an order

Dear Yusuf

1 It was a pleasure to meet you on Friday.

2 I am pleased to confirm that we would be able to give you a special price of £7,525 for the items you were considering which, as you can see, allows a very special discount. I have been assured that we would be able to arrange for delivery within 3-4 days of receiving your order.

3 I hope to receive your confirmation by return so that we can go ahead with this order on the terms agreed.

4 Please give me a call or fax me as soon as possible.

Yours sincerely

1 Refer to meeting.
2 Confirm price quoted and confirm special discount; mention delivery details
3 Request confirmation
4 Close

Follow-up after a meeting

Dear Miss Phillips

1 Thank you for visiting our stand at the Office 2000 Exhibition last week. I hope you found our representatives helpful.

2 On these occasions it is sometimes quite difficult to deal with specific queries due to the pressures at these events. However I am pleased to enclose our latest catalogue showing all our products, prices and terms.

3 Our representative in your area is William Tan and I have asked him to give you a call within the next few days. He will be pleased to arrange to visit you to discuss your requirements in more detail.

4 Meanwhile please do not hesitate to let me know if I can be of any further assistance.

Yours sincerely

1 Refer to meeting
2 Enclose further information
3 Mention representative's name and action to be taken
4 Courteous close

■ Form (see also REPLY FORM and TEAR-OFF SLIP)

Forms cannot be avoided in every aspect of our personal and business lives. Thoughtful design can make the job of completion so much easier. Here are some questions to consider when designing a form:

- Who will be completing the form?
- Who needs the information?
- Why is the information needed?
- How will the information be most effectively presented?
- What information will be needed? Write a checklist of headings.
- Can I divide the checklist into sub-sections? Give each one a title.
- What will be the most logical order for the information required?
- Should I use options boxes, yes/no or a space for insertion of information?
- How much space should be left for the required information?

Some well-designed forms are shown here (reproduced courtesy of Waterlow Business Supplies):

- Accident/Incident Report Form (see page 42)
- Interview Report Form (see pages 43–44)

1

ACCIDENT / INCIDENT REPORT FORM

2

It is good practice to keep a written record of any accident or incident, however minor, which occurs in the workplace. In any event there is a legal requirement that written records of 'reportable' accidents and dangerous occurrences (i.e. those which must be reported to the appropriate enforcing authority) be kept for a minimum of three years.

The accident log should be used to keep a record of all accidents/incidents which occur at the workplace, whether they are notifiable or not. Such a record can be used in a variety of ways: for example, if a claim of negligence is to be made against the employer the insurance company will require details of the accident. Management will need to see the record in order to take any necessary steps to try and reduce accidents in the future, such as issuing protective clothing. It may also be possible to identify a training need, closer supervision requirements or even accident proneness amongst particular employees.

3

Full name of person injured/involved ______________ Sex ☐ M ☐ F

Job Title ______________ Department ______________

Date and time of accident/incident ______________ Place of accident/incident ______________

4

Accident/Incident Occurred

- ☐ In normal working hours/overtime
- ☐ On employer's premises
- ☐ Obeying instructions
- ☐ Outside working hours
- ☐ On other private/public property
- ☐ Disobeying instructions

Classification of Cause (full details page 4)

- ☐ Burn
- ☐ Electrical Shock
- ☐ Fall
- ☐ Health hazard
- ☐ Struck
- ☐ Trapped
- ☐ Mechanical
- ☐ Other

____

5

Nature of Personal Injury

____

____

____

Sickness Benefit/Industrial Injury Benefit: ☐ Claimed ☐ Granted ☐ Terminated

Absence
Estimated length of absence from work ______________ Actual absence from work ______________

If employee returned to different employment specify nature and reason ______________

____

6

Medical Attention Given: ☐ by work's medical centre ☐ by doctor ☐ at hospital

Hospital Address ______________ Doctor Address ______________

______________ ______________

Telephone ______________ Telephone ______________

Means of transport to hospital and/or doctor ______________

Length of detention in hospital ______________

Hospital Patient No. ______________ ☐ X Ray X Ray Dept. No. ______________

Notification to:

- ☐ Safety Office Date ______________
- ☐ Union Officer Date ______________
- ☐ Accident Register Date ______________
- ☐ Safety Representative Date ______________
- ☐ Engineer Date ______________
- ☐ Enforcing Authority (Form F2508/F2508A) Date ______________

Scene Inspected ______________

____

PRINTED IN THE UK

FORM 125
10.95

1 Main heading
2 Some forms have an explanation at the top
3 Some statements require lines for completion
4 For others, tick boxes are better
5 Leave more space where more information is required (the second page of the form will provide more space)
6 Again another mix of lines/tick boxes

F

1

INTERVIEW REPORT

2

Name of applicant: ______________________________

Job applied for: ____________________ Reference: ____________________

Interviewer(s): ____________________ Date of interview: ____________________

Indicate your impressions gained from interviewing the applicant by ticking the appropriate box under each heading. Assess each attribute in relation to the job the candidate has applied for. Only assess if relevant.

3

1 Skills

☐ None appropriate	☐ Some skill in job area	☐ Reasonable amount; average for job	☐ Well skilled in job area	☐ Excellent skills; ideal for job

2 Knowledge of work field

4

☐ Poor; no appropriate knowledge at all	☐ Limited knowledge covering some areas	☐ Average knowledge not covering all areas fully	☐ Well informed; knowledge covers all areas	☐ Excellent level of knowledge

3 Experience

☐ No relation between background and job requirements	☐ Some experience in relevant area	☐ Average; background covers job area	☐ Very good and relevant experience	☐ Excellent and ideal background

4 Qualifications

☐ Not relevant to job	☐ Some relevance to job	☐ Satisfactory; as good as might be expected	☐ Very suitable for job	☐ Ideal for job; perfect match

5 Personality

☐ Unsatisfactory	☐ Doubtful	☐ Average and satisfactory	☐ Very good; above average	☐ Outstanding; excellent all round

6 Friendliness

☐ Appears very distant and aloof	☐ Reserved	☐ Approachable; fairly friendly	☐ Warm, friendly; sociable	☐ Extremely friendly; very warm and outgoing

FORM 103
7/94

1 Main heading
2 Allow sufficient space for completion of details
3 Use clear sub-headings
4 Tick boxes are used extensively on this form for ease of completion

7 Conversational ability

☐ Talks very little; poor expression	☐ Hesitant; lower than average fluency and expression	☐ Average fluency and expression	☐ Talks well and does not waste words	☐ Excellent expression; extremely fluent; forceful

8 Confidence

☐ Ill at ease; jumpy and very nervous	☐ Somewhat tense; easily irritated	☐ Reasonably at ease	☐ Self assured	☐ Extremely well composed

9 Drive and Initiative

☐ Poorly defined goals; acts without purpose	☐ Makes little effort to achieve goals	☐ Average effort; some initiative	☐ High desire to achieve; strives hard	☐ Sets high goals; always takes initiative

5

10 Alertness

☐ Very slow to grasp ideas	☐ Rather slow; requires more than average explanation	☐ Grasps ideas with average speed	☐ Quick to understand; perceives well	☐ Exceptionally alert; understands new ideas instantly

11 Appearance

☐ Very untidy	☐ Somewhat careless about personal appearance	☐ Satisfactory personal appearance	☐ Neat and tidy; better than average appearance	☐ Unusually well groomed and very neat

12 Overall

☐ Unsatisfactory	☐ Below standard, but just acceptable	☐ Average	☐ Above average; higher than required standard	☐ Outstanding

Reasons and comments: ____________________

6

This applicant should be:
☐ offered the job
☐ considered for further interview
☐ placed on 'hold'
☐ rejected

Signature of Interviewer____________________

5 The 5 sections have been carefully worded under each heading

6 A section is provided for general comments to be made

■ Fully blocked layout (see BUSINESS LETTER LAYOUT)

G

■ Goodwill letter (see also APOLOGY, CONDOLENCE, CONGRATULATIONS, THANK YOU LETTER)

One of the most important functions of all business communications is to create good business relations. Every opportunity should be taken to write goodwill letters. They may be written on such occasions as:

- appreciation
- welcome
- promotion
- unwelcome news
- birth
- marriage
- death
- special award

Goodwill letters written on such occasions as these are very good for business. They strengthen existing relationships and they may also create new business opportunities. Goodwill letters should be written and sent promptly. Keep them brief, sincere and fairly informal. Where possible handwritten notes give an added touch of sincerity and intimacy.

Goodwill letter acknowledging an accomplishment

> Dear Graham
>
> [1] The first edition of our new company newsletter, *GLOBAL TIMES*, is superb.
>
> [2] It is very evident that you have put a great deal of time and thought into the contents and design of our newsletter. The articles are very interesting and informative and the photographs brought the news alive. You have done an excellent job of putting this together and should be very proud of such a professional result.
>
> [3] I am sure *GLOBAL TIMES* will be very successful and shall look forward to future editions.
>
> Yours sincerely

1 Immediate compliment
2 Personal feelings and comments
3 Final compliment

H

■ Handout (see also CHECKLIST)

When making a presentation or giving a lecture you will have to prepare handouts to issue to all participants. Handouts are useful for reference after your presentation. They should summarise the main points that you discussed. Sub-headings and numbered points are useful. Remember also grammatical parallelism – presenting each point in the same grammatical style.

1 Give a clear heading
2 A short introductory paragraph is a good idea
3 Use sub-headings and numbered points
4 This two-column format is useful
5 Starting each point with a verb ensures grammatical parallelism

1 **BUSINESS ENGLISH EXAMINATIONS**

How can you help yourself?

2 In Business English/Communication examinations there are often no right or wrong answers – only those that are businesslike, appropriate and accurate. Assessment will usually take into consideration various factors like language, content, layout, tone and style.

3 **General Guidelines**

1 Use a new page for each answer. Show the number clearly in the margin.

2 When handwriting answers, leave a line space between paragraphs just as you would when typing. Avoid cramping.

3 Align correctly when using numbered points.

4 Use capitals or underlining consistently.

5 Ensure that your handwriting is legible.

6 Go easy on the liquid correction fluid.

7 Check for accuracy in grammar, spelling and punctuation – and then check again!

4 **Comprehension**

1 Explain clearly and concisely, in your own words where possible.

5 2 Consider the contextual meanings when definitions are required.

3 Consider the marks available for each question.

Business Documents

1 Display business documents correctly and consistently, using the same style when handwriting documents as you would if typing them.

2 Include all mechanical details, eg letterhead, reference, date, subject heading, sender's name, title, enclosures, copies, etc.

3 Head continuation sheets appropriately.

4 Use a tone appropriate to the reader/sender/purpose.

5 Insert names, places, dates, etc to add realism to answers.

6 Structure documents logically, rearranging information provided – but make a plan first.

Summarising

1 Consider the purpose for which the summary is to be used.

2 Use a suitable format.

3 Use your own words wherever possible.

4 Do not use short note form unless instructed to do so.

5 Consider the word limit.

6 Include a covering memo when appropriate.

(Reproduced from *Communication for Business*, Third Edition)

I

■ Interview letter (see also APPOINTMENT LETTER, EMPLOYMENT APPLICATION, RESUMÉ)

A letter inviting an applicant for interview should be simple and specific as illustrated in this example.

> Dear Mrs Newman
>
> [1] TRAINER - COMMUNICATIONS
>
> [2] Thank you for your application for this post.
>
> [3] Please attend an interview with me and Mr Leslie Wong, Course Director (Communications), on Wednesday 25 August at 2.30 pm.
>
> [4] If you are unable to keep this appointment please telephone my secretary, Martha Lim, as soon as possible.
>
> Yours sincerely

1 Heading gives title of post
2 Refer to application
3 Give details of interview
4 Action in case of inconvenience

■ Introduction

Sometimes it is necessary to write a letter introducing someone in your organisation to someone he or she has to do business with. In such cases it is best to stick with the basic information and facts. It is fine to be enthusiastic but try not to oversell the person. They can do that for themselves.

Letter of introduction

> Dear Martin
>
> [1] [2] I would like to introduce our new Marketing Manager, Sarah Hillman, who joined us last week. Sarah has several years of experience in the telecommunications industry, and she comes to us very energetic and motivated for the exciting challenges ahead.
>
> [3] Sarah will be in touch with you soon to find out how we can work together with you over the next few months. I know you will find Sarah very friendly and enthusiastic, and hope you will make time to see her.
>
> Yours sincerely

1 Give name and title and state commencement date
2 Give details of experience and qualities
3 Action to be taken

I

■ Invitation

Many companies organise special functions to publicise special events, for example the retirement of a senior executive, the opening of a new branch, a special anniversary. Formal invitations are printed on A4 or A5 good quality paper or card.

Invitation to special anniversary celebration

1 The Directors of
Global Technology Pte Ltd
have pleasure in inviting

2 ……………………………………………………………

3 to attend their 25th Anniversary Celebration
to be held at

4 The Orchid Suite
Pagoda Hotel
Nathan Road
Hong Kong

5 on Friday 20 August 200-

6 Cocktails at 1930
Dinner at 2000

7 The Directors
Global Technology Pte Ltd
14 Lorong Mambong
Kowloon
Hong Kong

8 RSVP by 15 July 200-

1 Who is giving the invitation?
2 Leave a blank for name to be handwritten
3 State the occasion
4 Give full address
5 Include the date
6 Mention the timing
7 Address for reply
8 Date by which replies must be received

Reply to formal invitation

1 Mr Low Chwee Leong

of

2 LCL Electrical Supplies

3 thanks the Directors of Global Technology Pte Ltd

for their kind invitation to their
4 25th Anniversary Celebration

to be held at the Pagoda Hotel

on Friday 20 August 200-

5 and has much pleasure in attending

6 24 Peak Hill
Hong Kong

7 2 July 200_

1 Who is the reply from?
2 State the company's name too
3 Express thanks
4 Use the same format as original invitation
5 Use third person – accept the invitation
6 Your address
7 Date

Informal invitation

Invitations may also be presented in the form of an informal letter (see PERSONAL LETTER). Remember to reply in a similar manner.

1 — 29 Hope Street
Aston
Sheffield S26 2ES

2 —

3 — Can you believe we are still together after 25 years! We are extremely proud to announce that we will be celebrating our Silver Wedding Anniversary on Friday 11 August. In many respects it still seems like yesterday when we were married on the paradise island of Antigua.

4 — We are celebrating this special occasion by holding a party at our home from 1830 on our anniversary day.

We both sincerely hope that you will be able to join us to celebrate this special occasion.

5 —

1 Personal address at right or centre
2 Leave a blank to handwrite the salutation
3 Keep it friendly and informal
4 Give all details of day, date, time and place
5 Sign all invitations personally

Letter inviting a speaker to a conference

Dear Miss Forrester

1 We are planning to hold a one day seminar for our secretarial and administrative staff on Wednesday 24 June 2001. This will be held at the Juniper House Hotel, Bedford. Approximately 50 participants are expected to attend comprising practising secretaries, some administrators and clerks.

2 I know you have helped us by speaking at several of our inhouse training sessions. We should once again be delighted if you would accept our invitation to speak on the subject of 'Effective Business Writing'. This will be the second session of the day, from 1100 to 1200. We would be able to pay you the fee of £100 and of course your travel expenses. Accommodation can be arranged for you on the previous evening if required.

3 A copy of the draft programme is enclosed, and you are welcome to attend any of the other sessions if you wish.

4 I really hope you will be able to accept this invitation. Please let me know as soon as possible, and at the same time please indicate any visual aids or other equipment you will need.

Yours sincerely

1 State function, date, venue and audience
2 Refer to previous collaboration; give timing and reimbursement details
3 Enclose draft programme
4 Request confirmation of acceptance and other information needed

■ Itinerary

An itinerary gives full details of a journey in order of date. It shows all travel arrangements, accommodation and appointments.

1 MR EDWARD TAN

PROVISIONAL ITINERARY
VISIT TO SINGAPORE 16-29 JUNE 2000

2 SATURDAY 16 JUNE

2230	Depart London Heathrow (SQ 227)

SUNDAY 17 JUNE

3 1830	Arrive Singapore Changi Airport (Terminal 2)
	Accommodation: Raffles Hotel

MONDAY 18 JUNE

4 1200	Lunch with Mandy Wong, Regional Manager, Global Singapore
1530	Visit to Singapore offices

TUESDAY 19 JUNE

1000-1800	International Conference - Day 1
	Jasmine Suite, Hyatt Hotel

5 WEDNESDAY 20 JUNE

1000-1700	International Conference - Day 2
	Jasmine Suite, Hyatt Hotel

6 THURSDAY 21 JUNE (Appointments with Mandy Wong)

1030	Martin Cheong, Manager, Jasper Communications (Jurong)
1400	Jane Lim, Manager, Network First (Holland Village)

FRIDAY 22 JUNE
Free day

MONDAY 25 JUNE and TUESDAY 26 JUNE

Meetings at Global offices (to be confirmed)

WEDNESDAY 27 JUNE

7 2230	Depart Singapore (SQ 228)

THURSDAY 28 JUNE

0830	Arrive London Heathrow

ET/ST
3 May 2000

1 Name and place/date covered in itinerary
2 Day and date in capitals as shoulder headings
3 Use two column format for ease of reference
4 Give details of all meetings
5 Be consistent in display of day/dates
6 Use 24 hour clock for times
7 Include flight numbers

■ Jargon (see also ABC OF GOOD BUSINESS WRITING, LANGUAGE, TERMINOLOGY, TONE)

Jargon means the terminology belonging to a particular activity or field. It has also come to mean a long-winded verbose style of writing which adds nothing to the meaning of what is written. People use a lot of jargon in business letters without really knowing why, but steps should be taken to eliminate it from modern business language.

Expressions which should be avoided in your business documents

Don't say:	**Say this instead:**
I enclose herewith	I enclose
Enclosed herewith you will find	I enclose
Please find enclosed	I enclose
Regarding this above-mentioned	Regarding this matter Regarding this post Regarding your application
We are in receipt of your letter.	Thank you for your letter of 21 June.
These goods are being sent under separate cover.	These goods are being sent separately.
Please be good enough to advise me	Please let me know
I would like to remind you that	Please remember that
We shall be in a position to	We shall be able to

Expressions which should be avoided

I have noticed that
It has come to my attention that
I am pleased to inform you that
I am writing to let you know that
I must inform you that
Will you please
Thanking you in anticipation
Thank you and regards
Kindest regards

■ Job description

A job description gives details of the duties and responsibilities involved in a post, including any supervisory duties, specific authority and any special features of the post.

1 Apollo Communications

JOB DESCRIPTION

2 JOB TITLE — Senior Secretary

REPORTS TO — Training Manager

LOCATION — Head Office, Sheffield

MAIN PURPOSE — To provide a confidential secretarial and support service to the Training Manager

REQUIREMENTS

3
1 Abilities: use initiative, decide priorities, work without supervision
2 Previous experience at senior level
3 Skills: Microsoft Office, notetaking skills, minute-taking skills, good organiser, good interpersonal skills
4 High standard of education with appropriate secretarial/administration qualifications

MAIN DUTIES AND RESPONSIBLITIES

4
1 To provide secretarial support to the Training Manager.
2 To deal with mail, answer telephone enquires, take messages and compose correspondence.
3 To take shorthand dictation and deal with instructions from manuscript, audio or disk and to transcribe documents accurately and consistently.

5
4 To maintain the diary of the Training Manager.
5 To arrange meetings and produce accurate minutes.
6 To arrange training courses and seminars.
7 To make travel and accommodation arrangements as required.
8 To ensure the security of the office and confidential documents.

6
9 To carry out any other duties as may be expected in a post of this level.

ST/BT
June 200_

1 If plain paper is used include the company's name. Sometimes letterheaded paper is used
2 Use appropriate headings relevant to the post
3 Sometimes specific requirements of the post holder are included
4 List the main duties and responsibilities
5 Make sure all points are expressed in a consistent style (eg 'To...')
6 Finish with this standard clause

K

■ KISS – Keep It Short and Simple (see also ABC OF GOOD BUSINESS WRITING, JARGON, LANGUAGE, TERMINOLOGY, TONE)

As you work to improve your business writing, remember this acronym – KISS. It stands for Keep It Short and Simple. Busy business men and women do not have time for long-winded writing. The essence of good business writing today is to keep it to the bare essentials. You must get to the point in the quickest possible way, while retaining courtesy of course. A good way to figure out whether something should be included or not is to ask yourself 'Would I SAY this?' The rule is . . . if you would not say it, don't write it!

Take a look at these examples.

Non-KISSable:	**Very KISSable:**
come to an agreement	agree
make an application	apply
arrived at the conclusion	concluded
give consideration to	consider
conduct an investigation	investigate
extend an invitation	invite
hold a meeting	meet
with reference to	regarding
give an indication of	show
at the earliest possible date	soon
I would like to take this opportunity to thank you	thank you

Remember that even when your message is quite long, your sentences should always be concise. Concise is not the opposite of long – it is the opposite of wordy. Here are some examples.

Non-KISSable	**KISSable**
I have received and read your letter dated Friday 28 June and wish to say that there is much truth in each and every statement that you make, and I fully understand and appreciate your position. (36 words)	Thank you for your letter of 28 June. I understand your views completely. (13 words)
The directors and I would greatly appreciate any ideas or suggestions that you are able to provide, and can assure you that they will all be given our fullest attention and consideration. (32 words)	Please send us your ideas. We will give then our full consideration. (12 words)

Language (see also ABC OF GOOD BUSINESS WRITING, JARGON, TERMINOLOGY, TONE)

When writing any business letter, memo or other document, you should aim to put your message across in a natural way. It is common business practice to use an informal style of writing, as if you are having 'a conversation in writing' rather than being too formal. Effective written communication results when you say exactly what you want to say using appropriate business language, tone and manner.

Be courteous and considerate

Writing in a courteous style enables a request to be refused without ruining all hope of future business. It also allows a refusal to be made without ruining a friendship. Courtesy also means:

1 Reply promptly to all communications – on the same day if possible.
2 If an immediate answer is impossible, write a brief note and explain why.
3 Try to appreciate and respect the recipient's point of view.
4 Never reply in such a tone that you imply that your correspondent is wrong.
5 Even if you feel someone's comments are unfair, be tactful and try not to give offence.
6 Resist the temptation to reply to an offensive letter in a similar tone. Answer courteously without lowering your dignity.

Use simple words

Take care to avoid using long-winded, old-fashioned words and phrases in modern business communications. Such language very often leads to confusion. Using short simple words will help you put your message over more efficiently and effectively.

Don't say:	Say this instead:
with reference to	about
due to the fact that	because
take into consideration	consider
enclosed herewith	enclosed
with the exception of	except
for the purpose of	for
in the event that	if, when
in the meantime	meanwhile
at the present time	now, currently, today
under separate cover	separately
purchase	buy
sufficient	enough
remittance	payment
endeavour	try
advise, inform	tell
forward, transmit	send
expedite	speed up, hurry

Write naturally and sincerely

Try to show a genuine interest in the recipient and their problems. Your message should sound sincere while being written in your own unique style. Write naturally, as if you were having a conversation.

Don't say this:	Say this instead:
I have pleasure in informing you …	I am pleased to tell you …
We do not anticipate any increase in prices.	We do not expect prices to rise.
I should be grateful if you would be good enough to advise us …	Please let us know …
Please favour us with a prompt reply.	I hope to hear from you soon.

■ Leaflet

Leaflets or flyers are often used to publicise goods or services, to promote special events and promotions or to give information of any kind. Leaflets may be in the form of a single page or they could be folded once or twice, as shown in these illustrations:

Leaflets should make effective use of sub-headings, numbered points, bullets and/or illustrations, as shown in this example.

1 *Most infections get better without antibiotics*

In cases where patients will get better without antibiotics, it makes sense for your doctor not to prescribe them. Your body's defence system can often protect against infection without the need for antibiotics.

2 **Listen to your doctor**

Your doctor will be able to recognise whether you have an infection that needs antibiotics, so you should not always expect to be given a prescription. Doctors need to prescribe antibiotics with care. This is because inappropriate use of antibiotics can be dangerous for individual patients and for the whole population.

Overuse of antibiotics can also cause resistance and result in them not working in the future. This is a very worrying trend, especially for patients with serious life-threatening infections.

- There are effective alternative remedies for managing the symptoms of many infections.

3 **If you are prescribed antibiotics ensure you take the medication according to instructions.**

- Although you may begin to feel better, you must take the full course of antibiotics to prevent your illness coming back.
- Not taking the full course of antibiotics can lead to future antibiotic resistance.

1 Snappy headline giving the gist at a glance
2 Use sub-headings to break up information according to different aspects of the main theme
3 Important sections may be boxed for extra emphasis

Harmful side-effects

Potential side-effects are another reason why doctors are cautious about prescribing antibiotics. Some antibiotic treatment can cause side-effects such as stomach upset and thrush. For women on the pill antibiotics can reduce contraceptive protection

Antibiotic facts

4 • Antibiotics have no effect on viral infections (e.g. colds, flu and most sore throats). Viral infections are much more
5 common than bacterial infections.
- Inappropriate use of antibiotics can encourage the development of resistant bacteria. This could mean that the antibiotic may not work when you really need it.

6 • Some antibiotics have harmful side-effects such as diarrhoea and allergic reactions.
- Antibiotics do not just attack the infection they are prescribed for – they can also kill useful bacteria which normally protect you against other infections such as thrush.

If you have an infection such as a cold, flu or sore throat

- Take paracetamol according to the instruction to help reduce fever and relieve aches and pains.
- Drink plenty of water to avoid dehydration
- Ask your pharmacist (*chemist*) for advice. Many infections can be managed effectively with over-the-counter medications. The pharmacist will refer you to your doctor or practice nurse if they think it is necessary.

When to contact your GP

Call your GP's surgery for advice if, after taking over-the-counter medications, as directed, you or your child are experiencing any of the following:

- symptoms which are severe or unusually prolonged
- extreme shortness of breath
- coughing up of blood or large amounts of yellow or green phlegm.

DOCTOR PATIENT PARTNERSHIP

Promoting a healthy partnership between
7 *patients and health professionals*

BMA House Tavistock Square London WC1H 9JP
Fax: 0171 383 6403 Internet: www.doctorpatient.org.uk

4 Use bullet points where possible
5 Use everyday language, and simple expressions
6 Aim for an effective and attractive display which uses space to advantage
7 Include company name, address and contact details

M

■ Memo

A memorandum (or memo) is a written communication from one person to another (or to a group of people) within the same organisation. Many companies use standard memo forms, but generally the fully-blocked style can be used for memos as with all business documents. When more than one topic is dealt with, as is often the case with memos, use numbered points and sub-headings. It is not general practice to include a salutation or complimentary close on memos, but they are usually signed or initialled.

Memo requesting agenda items

MEMORANDUM

To Departmental Heads

1 From Steven Broom, Administration Manager

Ref SB/ST

Date 2 July 200_

2 OPERATIONS MEETING – 14 JULY

3 Please note that the next Operations Meeting will be held in the Conference Room at 1000 hours on Monday 14 July.

Follow-up items from our last meeting which will be included under Matters Arising are:

4
- New brochure (Suzanne Sutcliffe)
- Annual Dinner and Dance (Mandy Lim)

5 If you wish to add any further items to the agenda please let me know before 8 July.

1 Display memo headings in the usual way
2 Heading states name and date of meeting
3 Clarify meeting, venue, time and date of meeting
4 Mention any items already included on the agenda
5 Give a deadline for submission of extra items

Memo explaining document layout to new assistant

1 **MEMORANDUM**

2 *To* Mandy Lim, Administrative Assistant
3 *From* Sally Thomas, PA to Chairman
4 *Ref* ST/JJ
5 *Date* 14 August 200_

6 INHOUSE DOCUMENT FORMATS

7 Many congratulations on recently joining the staff in the Chairman's office. I hope you will be very happy here.

I am enclosing a booklet explaining the company's general rules regarding document formats. However, I thought it would be helpful if I summarised the rules for ease of reference.

1 DOCUMENT FORMATS
8 All documents should be presented in the fully-blocked format using open punctuation. Specimen letters, fax messages, memoranda and other documents are included in the booklet. These examples should guide you in our requirements.

2 SIGNATURE BLOCK (LETTERS)
In outgoing letters it is usual practice to display the sender's name in capitals and the title directly underneath in lower case with initial capitals.

3 NUMBERED ITEMS
In reports and other documents it is often necessary to number items. In such cases the numbers should be displayed alone with no full stops or brackets. Subsequent numbering should be decimal, ie 3.1, 3.2, etc.

9 I hope these guidelines will be useful and that you will study the layouts shown in your booklet. If you have any questions please do not hesitate to ask me.

10 *Sally Thomas*

11 Enc

12 Copy: Personnel Department

1 Emphasise the word MEMORANDUM
2 Insert the recipient's name and designation
3 The sender's name and designation
4 A reference (initials of sender and typist)
5 Date of issue
6 No salutations necessary
7 Subject heading – clearly state the topic of the message
8 The body of the memo should be separated into paragraphs, reaching a relevant conclusion and close
9 No complimentary close is necessary
10 Leave space for signature (The sender's name and designation are at the top so it is not necessary to repeat these details here
11 Enc (if appropriate)
12 Copy (if appropriate)

Memo including agenda

MEMORANDUM

1 To Departmental Managers

From Steven Broom, Administration Manager

Ref SE/ST

Date 2 July 200_

OPERATIONS MEETING

2 The next monthly Operations Meeting will be held in the Conference Room at 1000 hrs on Monday 14 July 200_.

3 AGENDA

4 1 Apologies for absence

2 Minutes of last meeting

3 Matters arising

3.1 New brochure (Suzanne Sutcliffe)

3.2 Annual Dinner and Dance (Mandy Lim)

4 New branches (Suzanne Sutcliffe)

5 5 Far East Trip (Sally Turner)

6 European Telecommunications Conference (John Stevens)

7 5th Anniversary Celebrations (Suzanne Sutscliffe)

6 8 Any other business

9 Date of next meeting

1 Display memo headings in the usual way
2 Confirm details regarding venue, date and time
3 State the word AGENDA
4 These first 3 items of 'ordinary business' should be included on every agenda
5 These are items of 'special' business', specific to this meeting only
6 These final 2 items are again 'ordinary business'

■ Minutes

Minutes are a written record of what took place at a meeting. An accurate written record is essential not only for those who attended the meeting but also for those who were unable to attend. Minutes should be written in the past tense using the third person and reported speech.

There are three main types of minutes.

1 Verbatim minutes

These are used primarily in court reporting where every word needs recording exactly as it is spoken.

2 Minutes of resolution

Resolution minutes do not include a note of the discussions which took place, only the main conclusions reached at the meeting. Resolution minutes are usually used for minutes of Annual General Meetings and other statutory meetings.

Example

REFURBISHMENT OF GENERAL OFFICE

The Company Secretary submitted a report from the Administration Manager containing full details of the proposed refurbishment of the general office, together with an estimate from GYK Builders.

IT WAS RESOLVED THAT GYK Builders should be asked to carry out the work at the estimated cost of £25,500.

3 Minutes of narration

Narrative minutes will be a concise summary of all the discussions which took place, reports received, actions to be taken and decisions made. The example of the minutes shown here is written in narrative style.

1 Company name
2 Heading includes place, day, date and time of meeting
3 List people present in alphabetical order with Chairman first
4 Follow the order of the agenda
5 Previous minutes must be corrected before they can be signed
6 State any matters arising from previous minutes
7 Include initials or names of people who have to take action
8 Use past tense and reported speech in minutes
9 Leave space for Chairman to sign and date at next meeting

Minutes of a Meeting of the Social Committee

1 GLOBAL COMMUNICATIONS plc

2 MINUTES of a meeting held in the Training Room at 1030 on Friday 4 February 2000

PRESENT Mrs Sally Turner (Chairman)
3 Mr Robert Manley
Miss Rita Ong
Mrs Penny Wilson

4 1 APOLOGIES FOR ABSENCE
Apologies were received from Mrs Clare Green who was on holiday.

2 MINUTES OF LAST MEETING
5 In Item 3 the figure £45.50 was corrected to read £450.50. After this correction was made the minutes were signed by the Chairman as a correct record.

3 MATTERS ARISING
6 There were no matters arising.

4 RETIREMENT CELEBRATION OF PETER ONG, MARKETING DIRECTOR

4.1 VENUES
Various venues were suggested for this celebration to be held on Friday 14 August 2000. Penny Wilson agreed to contact the Regal Prince Hotel which had recently added a new wing of banqueting facilities. PW

7 4.2 INVITATIONS
It was decided that all staff would be invited, but not partners. Rita Ong agreed to draw up a list of 30 special guests. She will also design a formal invitation. Replies to be requested by the end of July. RO

4.3 PROGRAMME
Sally Turner issued a provisional programme and this was agreed. She will contact the relevant executives with regard to their participation and speeches. ST

5 NEWSLETTER
8 A draft of the new company newsletter was issued and discussed. It was agreed that Robert Manley and staff in his department had made a fabulous job of designing this inaugural newsletter. After various amendments and suggestions were made, Robert was asked to proceed with publication. RM

6 ANY OTHER BUSINESS
There was no other business

7 DATE OF NEXT MEETING
It was agreed that the next meeting would be held on Friday 28 February 2000.

.... Chairman
9
.... Date

ST/JL
7 February 2000

M

N

■ Newsletter (see also ARTICLE)

Many companies keep staff informed about matters of interest by issuing a regular staff newsletter. This may be published monthly or quarterly. Newsletters may contain articles on a variety of different issues including:

- new policies/procedures
- updates on products/services
- births/marriages/deaths
- weddings
- promotions
- sports and social news
- contributions from employees
- competitions

Some companies also produce newsletters especially for customers or members of a certain industry. These newsletters are a good way of keeping people informed about the latest products, news and developments within specific sectors of the industry.

■ No Thank You Letter (see REFUSAL)

■ Notice

Most organisations have notice boards at prominent places around the offices. These are used to bring special items to the attention of all staff. Notices may be posted about:

- new procedures
- social events
- advertisements for internal appointments
- reports on matters of interest

Information on a notice must be displayed attractively so that it gains attention and receives co-operation. The main points to remember when designing a notice are highlighted in this example:

1 CAN YOU ACT?

(OR WOULD YOU LIKE TO TRY?)

2 This year Global Communications celebrates its 10th year of providing quality telecommunications equipment. To mark this special occasion we are holding a 10th Anniversary Celebration at the Regal Prince Hotel in July. Special guests, directors and staff are to be invited.

3 A special 20-minute sketch has been written and we are now looking for aspiring actors and actresses to perform the sketch.

4 INTERESTED?

If you would like to attend an audition for a part in this sketch please come along and find out more.

When? Monday 15 March

5 Where? Training Room, Global House

Time? 6.00 - 8.00 pm

If you will be coming along to the auditions please call Mandy Jones, Marketing Department, to put your name down.

6 James Porter
Marketing Manager

JP/ST
7 2 March 2000

1 Headline to draw attention
2 Make it sound interesting
3 Give full details
4 Use another heading if relevant
5 Use attractive layout to draw attention to special points
6 Include name/title at foot of notices
7 Always date notices

O

■ Offer of appointment (see APPOINTMENT LETTER)

■ Open punctuation

When using the fully blocked layout it is most common to use open punctuation. Only punctuation marks which are essential for grammatical accuracy are included within the text of correspondence. All other commas and full stops are omitted. Always be consistent when using open punctuation. Remember to use open punctuation in:

• **Dates**	8 August 2000
• **Names**	Mr & Mrs N S Taylor
• **Addresses**	Mrs Mary Watkins 14 Hunter Avenue Shelf Halifax HX14 8TJ
• **Salutation and complimentary close**	Dear Mary Yours sincerely
• **Abbreviations**	Mr BEd RSA Mrs IBM LCCIEB NB MRT SIA

P

■ Personal letter

When preparing a personal letter your home address will be placed at the top right hand side. Every line may be flush with the right-hand margin or all lines may start at the same point, as in the example shown. Remember that the rest of the letter will be fully-blocked at the left margin. Presenting your personal address at the top right will just give a nice balanced appearance.

Display of personal letter

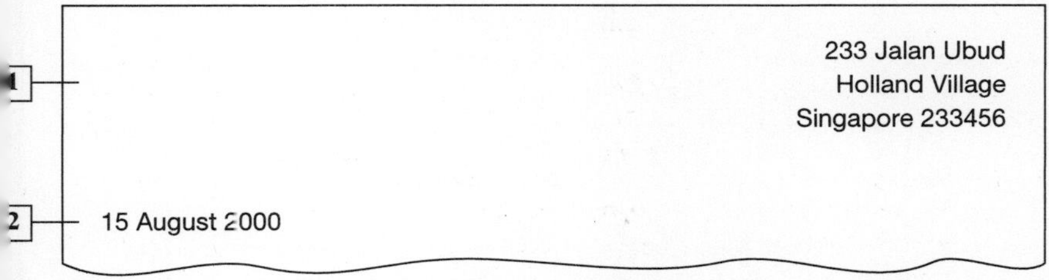

1 Your address at the right (or in centre)
2 Date at left margin (and fully block the rest)

■ Press release (see also ARTICLE)

A press release is an announcement sent to the press and other media about something which is considered to be newsworthy. Some reasons for issuing a press release may be:

- Expansion of business
- Management changes
- New premises
- New products
- Special projects or functions

If the article is published it can result in useful publicity but it must be remembered that a press release is not an advertisement or an invitation. When writing your press release try to imagine you are the editor of the newspaper and write in third person, reported speech.

Apollo Communications Mobile Phone specialists

21 Ashton Drive
Sheffield
S26 2ES

Tel +44 114 2871122
Fax +44 114 2871123
Email Apollo@A-Z.com.uk

ST/BT

1 15 June 200_

2 PUBLICATION DATE: Immediate

3 NEW JOBS IN APOLLO SUPERSTORE

4 Mobile phone specialists, Apollo Communications, have today announced the opening of their new store Apollo's Office Supplies. More than 50 new jobs have been created.

5 Apollo Communications have established themselves as leaders in the field of mobile communications in the UK. Roaming agreements have been set up with many countries throughout the world.

6 The company has now announced that it is diversifying. Its new Office Supplies superstore will sell everything from stationery and office sundries to computers and other office equipment. It will be situated in a prime location at Meadowhall Retail Park on the outskirts of Sheffield, very close to the M1 motorway.

A grand opening ceremony is planned to take place on Monday 1 July with special offers to the first 100 customers and a grand draw at 5.00 pm.

7 Sally Turner, Managing Director, said 'We are very excited about this new office superstore and feel confident that it will prove to be an overwhelming success.'

8 Contact: Diana Wilson, Marketing Manager, Apollo Communications
Telephone: 0114 2871222

1 Include reference and date
2 The embargo date is the date before which the information cannot be published
3 Give it a snappy headline
4 Introduction; state the main message quickly
5 Use short, self-contained paragraphs – include all essential details
6 Use double spacing for the press release
7 Round it off with a conclusion or quotation
8 State contact details (for further information/photographs)

■ Programme

When organising any function a provisional programme is usually drafted. This can be discussed and then confirmed nearer the date. Programmes should be displayed in 2 columns (or more if relevant) and it is usual for the 24-hour clock to be used.

Programme for 10th Anniversary Celebration

P

1 GLOBAL COMMUNICATIONS

10TH ANNIVERSARY CELEBRATION

2 to be held on Friday 12 July 2000 at Orchid Suite
Regal Prince Hotel
Kowloon
Hong Kong

3 PROGRAMME

4 1800	Arrival of Global Communications directors and staff
1830	Arrival of special guests Staff of the Administration Department will issue name tags and folders to all guests on arrival. They will be shown into the Orchid Suite. Cocktails will be served as guests arrive.
5 1900	Introduction by Master of Ceremonies (Peter Lim, Administration Director)
6 1910	Happy 10th Birthday Global Communications – a special 20 minute video
1930	Opening address by Chairman, Michael Hunter
2000	Buffet supper
2100	Sketch by Global staff
2130	Toasts by David Garson, Public Relations Director
2145	Closing address by Alan Robinson, Managing Director 7 Drinks will be served until 2230

PL/ST
3 March 2000

1 Company name and heading
2 Day/date and venue
3 State whether provisional or not
4 Use 24-hour clock
5 Use two-column format for ease of reference
6 State each item separately
7 Mention finishing time

Q

■ **Questionnaire** (see also FORM, REPLY FORM, TEAR-OFF SLIP)

Questionnaires are widely used in business. They are a special type of form designed to record opinions or suggestions. In many respects the design of questionnaires is even more important than ordinary forms because it is not compulsory to fill in questionnaires – it is completely up to the public whether or not they wish to fill them in.

When designing a questionnaire, different techniques can be used for asking questions. Several techniques are illustrated in this questionnaire:

About Prime

Is this the first time you have bought Prime?

❍ Yes ❍ No

Where did you first hear about Prime?

❍ Newspaper advertisement
❍ Newspaper article
❍ Magazine advertisement
❍ Magazine feature
❍ Saw in-store
❍ Radio
❍ TV
❍ Friend's recommendation
❍ Chemist's recommendation
❍ Doctor's recommendation

In which type of shop did you buy Prime?

❍ Healthfood store ❍ Chemist ❍ Other

Why did you buy Prime? ....

....

Have you previously bought other products for this reason?

❍ Yes ❍ No

If yes, which product and why? ....

....

Are you satisfied with Prime?

❍ Very satisfied ❍ Satisfied ❍ Dissatisfied ❍ Not sure

Would you buy Prime again?

❍ Yes ❍ Maybe ❍ Not sure ❍ No

If no, why? ....

How much do you spend on supplements each month? ....

Please tell us about yourself.

❍ Male ❍ Female

Mr/Mrs/Miss/Ms .... Name ....

Address ....

....

Age ❍ –25 ❍ 26–35 ❍ 36–45
❍ 46–60 ❍ 61+

Your occupation

❍ Professional ❍ Retired
❍ Administration ❍ Unemployed
❍ Manual ❍ Student

Data protection: The information you provide will be treated in strict confidence and will not be linked with your name. Relevant data will be recorded on our database. Information will not be rented out or released to other companies.

Thank you for completing our questionnaire.

Please send to: Global Healthcare Ltd, FREEPOST,
Sheffield S26 2ES (No stamp required)

R

■ Recruitment letter (see EMPLOYMENT APPLICATION, INTERVIEW LETTER, REFERENCE, RESUMÉ, TESTIMONIAL)

■ Redundancy

Redundancy (sometimes referred to as retrenchment) may result after company reorganisation when certain jobs or departments may no longer exist. This is always a sensitive issue. Before making any decision on redundancy you must be sure of the legal implications, as well as any trade union requirements. Make sure you also check financial compensation requirements required by law.

Wherever possible a letter regarding impending redundancy should be written after a meeting where the issue can be discussed personally and compassionately. Small-scale redundancies are sometimes made on a 'last in, first out' basis with recently employed staff having the least security. Sometimes employees may take voluntary redundancy, with the incentive of more generous compensation.

Letter explaining redundancy

Dear Mr Harrison

1 As you know the Board recently authorised an investigation by a firm of management consultants. They have made several recommendations which will result in reorganisation of our offices and therefore a decrease in the number of staff required.

2 Further to our meeting today it is with regret that I confirm that your position as Purchase Ledger Officer is one which will become redundant on 31 October. I hope that by giving you plenty of notice you will be able to find alternative employment without too much trouble.

3 A total of £6000 redundancy payment will be due to you. This has been calculated by taking one month's salary (at the rate effective when your services end) for each of your 6 years' service.

4 Your work has always been entirely satisfactory and I hope you can appreciate that I am taking this action with some regret. I shall be happy to provide any prospective employer with a reference if required.

5 I wish you every success in finding another suitable post, and best wishes for the future.

Yours sincerely

1 Background information
2 Express regret and state redundancy date
3 State redundancy payment and explain how it is calculated
4 Comment on work and refer to reference
5 Courteous close

R

Letter to several employees asking for volunteers for redundancy

Dear Mrs Graham

1 I am sure you realise that the company has been suffering recently from the economic downturn. Sales have fallen, costs have increased, and unfortunately we have not been making the profit which is necessary to keep our business healthy.

2 As a result I now have the unpleasant responsibility of reducing labour costs in this department. This inevitably means making a number of redundancies. Unfortunately I have to reduce staff in this department by 5.

In order to avoid imposing unnecessary hardship on any member of staff, it has been decided to give staff the opportunity to take voluntary redundancies.
3 Generous financial compensation will be given. This could be a good opportunity for those employees who may have thought of making a break or setting up on their own but always lacked the necessary finance.

4 I very much regret having to make this announcement, especially as so many of you have been with the company for several years. However in this present economic crisis I am afraid that there is very little choice. I do hope that the necessary redundancies can be achieved voluntarily. If you are interested please come and see me as soon as possible and we can discuss redundancy terms in confidence.

Yours sincerely

1 Background information
2 Express regret
3 Explain situation regarding voluntary redundancies
4 Express regret again and state action expected

■ Reference (see also TRADE REFERENCE)

If you are considering someone for a job it is usual to take up references. You may decide to do this on the telephone. However a more formal reply may be necessary through a written reference.

Letter requesting a reference

> Dear Mrs Richardson
>
> 1 Mrs Sylvia Lim has applied to us for the position of Executive Secretary to the Managing Director. This position calls for the expected standards of administrative and secretarial excellence, a high degree of confidentiality as well as an ability to supervise junior secretaries and undertake research tasks.
>
> 2 I should be grateful for any information you can give me about Mrs Lim's work performance, reliability and general character.
>
> 3 All information will be treated with the strictest confidence.
>
> Yours sincerely

1 State name and title; give background details
2 State information required
3 Give assurance of confidentiality

R

Reference

Dear Mr Wilson

1 Mrs Sylvia Lim was employed as Shorthand Typist in our Sales Department from September 1992 but was promoted to my Personal Assistant in 1996. She left the company in 1999 when she moved with her family to Aberdeen.

2 Her responsibilities included the usual secretarial duties as well as attending meetings, transcribing minutes and supervising and advising junior secretaries. It was also very often necessary for her to carry out research and produce reports and statistics on occasion, and Sylvia always enjoyed the challenge of such responsibilities. She headed a committee which organised the company's social functions.

3 Sylvia was always very conscientious in her work. She performed her work quickly and accurately and was always particularly meticulous in the presentation and layout of her work. I found her extremely well organised and skilled in handling the administration involved in her post. Sylvia is a capable, efficient secretary and an extremely skilful assistant.

4 Sylvia enjoyed good health and was a very good time-keeper. She had a friendly, outgoing personality and was very popular with clients and colleagues. It was a great loss to both myself and the company when Sylvia left the company.

5 I give Sylvia Lim my highest recommendation. I have no doubt that she would be a valuable member of your staff.

Yours sincerely

1. State name, title and dates of employment
2. Mention responsibilities undertaken
3. Discuss working attitude
4. Include personal qualities and feelings about employee leaving
5. Give a recommendation

■ Reference (unfavourable)

If you are asked for a reference for someone whose services have not been entirely satisfactory, it is generally safer to make unfavourable comments over the telephone or in person rather than in writing. If it is necessary for you to put an unfavourable reference in writing, be careful to use caution and restraint and give as little detail as possible.

A reference when you feel a new employer should be warned

> Dear Mr Richardson
>
> [1] Thank you for your letter of 25 August requesting a reference for Nigel Hamilton.
>
> [2] Mr Hamilton worked for this company as a Sales Representative for 6 years from June 1988 to October 1994. He was always punctual and enjoyed good health.
>
> [3] Please do not hesitate to give me a call if you require further details.
>
> Yours sincerely

1 Refer to letter.
2 Give title and period of employment; include brief details without commitment
3 Ask recipient to call you

Alternative unfavourable reference

> Dear Mr Shamlan
>
> [1] Thank you for your letter of 20 May enquiring about Mr Peter Wong.
>
> [2] Mr Wong was employed as Clerk in this company from March 1998 to October 1999. We released him because his work fell below the standards we normally expect. He also had quite a disturbing influence on other members of staff.
>
> [3] It is quite possible that with more self-discipline and maturity he could do better in another environment.
>
> Yours sincerely

1 Refer to letter
2 Give title and period of employment; state reason he was released
3 A courteous close giving employee the benefit of the doubt

■ Refusal

A refusal should be firm but polite, because you are refusing something that someone wants. If you don't care what the other person thinks or feels, then you may decide to be blunt, but a little courtesy doesn't cost anything.

A blunt refusal

> Dear Sir
>
> [1] Thank you for your proposal. We do not require your services.
>
> Yours faithfully

1 Just say no

A polite refusal

> Dear Mr Worthington
>
> [1] Thank you for your letter of 18 July enclosing your marketing proposal.
>
> [2] I have read your proposal with interest. However, after serious consideration I have decided not to go ahead with this project at the present time.
>
> Yours sincerely

1 Thank
2 Express interest but still say no

A reluctant refusal

> Dear Mr King
>
> [1] Thank you for your letter of 10 October offering special discounts on your products.
>
> [2] We would very much like to take advantage of this offer. Unfortunately, however, we do not have the necessary funds available at present.
>
> [3] If you have any similar offers in the future, please keep me informed.
>
> Yours sincerely

1 Thank
2 Express interest but explain why you cannot say yes
3 Ask to be kept informed of future offers

Refusal of credit

> Dear Mr Little
>
> 1 Thank you for your order number 234BT.
>
> 2 Unfortunately we do not have enough information at the moment to grant our usual credit terms. Our pro forma invoice is enclosed and your order will be shipped as soon as your payment is received.
>
> Yours sincerely

1 Thank
2 A polite refusal and alternative suggestion

R

■ Rejection of application (see also APPOINTMENT LETTER, INTERVIEW LETTER)

> Dear Miss Johnson
>
> 1 Thank you for recently attending an interview for the post of Personal Assistant.
>
> 2 I am sorry to have to inform you that we are unable to offer you this position. Although you have excellent qualifications we have decided to appoint someone with more experience.
>
> I feel sure that you will soon be successful in finding suitable employment.
>
> 3 With best wishes
>
> Yours sincerely

1 Refer to interview
2 Express regret; state reason
3 Courteous close

■ Reply form (see also FORM, QUESTIONNAIRE, TEAR-OFF SLIP)

On many occasions in business replies are required from recipients of letters. If the information required is too much for a tear-off slip a separate reply form may be necessary. Take care to design the reply form carefully, and perhaps try it out on some colleagues, so that you do not encounter problems later.

Reply form for use internally

1 REPLY FORM

2a Please return by 31 July to Mr Mark Johnson
2b Administration Officer
Human Relations Department

3 INHOUSE TRAINING COURSES – AUTUMN 2001

4 1 I will/will not* be able to attend the training course for Managers on 21 October 1999.

2 Please enrol the following employees from this department on the courses named (continue overleaf if necessary):

Name Course

....

5

....

....

....

Signature .... Date ....

6 Name .... Title ....

Department .... Extension ....

7 * Please delete where applicable

1 Heading
2 (a) Reply date (b) Reply address (only title/dept needed when for internal use)
3 Use same heading as covering memo
4 Use numbered points if appropriate
5 Double space for completion
6 Include relevant details at the foot
7 Include this standard phrase where appropriate

Reply form for use externally

1 REPLY FORM

2a Please return by 18 March 2001 to: Mr John Kelly
Training Consultant
Global Training Enterprises
2b 123 Aurora Avenue
Westlake
Singapore 234828 or fax to us on 7822747

3 TWO-DAY CONFERENCE – 22/23 APRIL 2001
EFFECTIVE BUSINESS WRITING

1 I would like to attend this two-day conference.

4 2 I require accommodation on
❑ Thursday 21 April
5 ❑ Friday 22 April
❑ Saturday 23 April (please tick)

3 Payment method:
❑ My cheque for $600 is enclosed (payable to Global Training Enterprises).
OR
❑ Please charge my credit card with $600.

6 Card type (eg Visa/Amex/Master Card) ....

Expiry Date .... Card Name ....

7 Signature .... Date ....

Name (in capitals) ....

8 Title ....

Company ....

Address ....

....

.... Post code ....

Telephone .... Fax ....

1 Heading
2 (a) Reply date (b) Full address needed when used externally
3 Use same heading as covering letter/fax
4 Use numbered points for clarity
5 Use tick boxes where appropriate
6 Leave sufficient space for completion
7 Always include space for signature and date on all forms
8 When used externally include space for address etc

R

■ Report

Many different types of report are used in business, some quite short and informal and others fairly lengthy and formal. The ultimate purpose of any report is to provide the foundation for decisions to be made and action taken.

Some reports consist of no more than a simple statement recording an event, a visit or some circumstances with a note of action taken. Other reports include detailed explanations of facts, conclusions, and perhaps recommendations for future action. More detailed reports demand research which may involve interviews, visits, questionnaires and investigations. The information may be presented in written, tabular or graphic form and the writer would need to produce clear conclusions and recommendations.

Special writing skills are needed for writing reports. You must be able to:

- record facts clearly and objectively
- interpret information and make conclusions
- present suggestions on ways in which a situation may be improved

Reports demand much more attention than I am able to give them here. However in this section we will take a look at some fairly standard formal and informal reports.

A formal report (reproduced with permission from *Communication for Business* Third Edition)

1 **AURORA HOLDINGS**

REPORT ON COMPLAINTS ABOUT POOR SERVICE AND FOOD PROVIDED IN THE STAFF RESTAURANT

TERMS OF REFERENCE

2 To investigate complaints about poor service and food provided in the staff restaurant and to make recommendations, as requested by Mr Michael Lee, Administration Director, on 14 April 2000.

PROCEDURE

3 1 An interview was held with Mrs Alice Newton, Restaurant Manageress, on 15 April.

2 Interviews were held with a cross-section of staff (48) who used the restaurant between 15 and 20 April.

FINDINGS

4 1 INTERVIEW WITH RESTAURANT MANAGERESS

1.1 STAFFING

Mrs Newton has 3 full-time assistants. The youngest, Miss Lily Ng, attends day-release classes at Southpoint College on Monday, Wednesday and Friday each week. She works 1400–1700 on those days.

1.2 EQUIPMENT

A schedule of current equipment showing each item's year of purchase is attached. No problems were reported. However Mrs Newton said that additional equipment would be useful:

1 microwave oven
1 slow cooker
1 rice cooker

2 INTERVIEWS WITH STAFF

20 staff from the 1200–1300 lunch sitting were interviewed, and 28 from the 1300–1400 sitting.

1 Company's name and report title
2 Who asked for the report? What was requested? When was it requested?
3 List the steps taken to gather the information (use past tense)
4 Present the information obtained through each step mentioned in Procedure

R

5 — 2

6 — 2.1 CHOICE

The food available is shown on the attached schedule. 60% of the staff interviewed said they would prefer some cold meals to be provided. They said they may make alternative lunch arrangements if the variety does not improve.

2.2 QUEUING

70% of staff took lunch from 1200 to 1300 hours as opposed to 30% from 1300 to 1400. This resulted in large queues forming at the first lunch sitting.

CONCLUSIONS

7 — 1 There are insufficient assistants to cope with the preparation of food in the morning and with the popular first lunch sitting.

2 The present equipment is insufficient.

3 The selection of meals is not wide enough to cater for staff requirements.

4 The ratio of staff to each sitting is not balanced.

RECOMMENDATIONS

8 — 1 A new assistant should be recruited to work 0900–1400 hours on Monday, Wednesday and Friday.

2 Mrs Newton should be asked to devise some new dishes which also include cold choices.

3 Mrs Newton should be asked to look into prices and availability of the new equipment required.

4 The number of staff attending each sitting should be revised so that a more even balance can be achieved.

9 —

10 — TAN LAY HONG (Miss)
Business Administration Officer

ML/tlh

11 —

24 April 2000

5 Number second and subsequent pages
6 Use numbered points and sub-headings for clarity
7 What are the logical implications of the Findings?
8 What action do you suggest should be taken?
9 Sign the report here
10 Name and title of the writer
11 Reference and date

Memo report (reproduced with permission from *Communication for Business* Third Edition)

MEMORANDUM

1 To John McIver, Office Manager
From Ian Fisher, Administrative Assistant
Ref JM/IF
2 Date 5 August 2000

3 REPORT ON POOR TIME-KEEPING OF GENERAL OFFICE STAFF

4 Further to our meeting on 20 June I have investigated the complaints about time-keeping of staff in the general office. An interview was held with each of the 12 employees concerned. Their times of arrival over a 2-week period were noted.

1 PRIVATE TRANSPORT

5 Four members of staff travel to work by car. These employees were usually punctual and no problems were noted.

2 PUBLIC TRANSPORT

2.1 Eight members of staff travel to work on public transport, using the A25 bus from the town centre. These staff were often up to 15 minutes late, arriving at work around 0915.

2.2 The A25 bus should stop outside the office at 0855 but it was quite erratic in this respect. Its arrival varied from 0900 to 0910. The previous A25 bus from town arrived outside the office between 0830 and 0840.

3 CONCLUSIONS

6 The staff relying on public transport cannot be blamed for the late arrival of the A25 bus from town. They also cannot be expected to arrive 30 minutes early each day to avoid being a few minutes late for work. However changes in the office routine could help the problem.

4 RECOMMENDATIONS

7 The staff who use public transport should be given the option of starting work at 0845 and finishing 15 minutes earlier than usual.

I hope you find this report satisfactory. If you have any questions please let me know.

1 Names/titles of sender/recipient
2 Date report was written
3 Heading – specific and clear
4 Introduction – mention date report was requested and state steps taken
5 Findings – use sub-headings and numbered points; state results of your investigations; use past tense and reported speech
6 Conclusions – state the logical implications of the findings
7 Recommendations – if requested, suggest action

R

■ Reprimand (see WARNING LETTER)

■ Request for appointment (see also INVITATION)

Dear Mr Richards

1 Thank you for your letter dated 16 April regarding upgrading your household insurance.

2 I would like to visit you so that we can discuss this issue in detail. I will be in your area on Monday 15 August and hope it will be convenient if I call on you at 2.30 pm. If this will not be convenient please give me a call on 0114 2422342.

3 I look forward to seeing you then.

Yours sincerely

1 Refer to letter
2 Mention day, date and time; give number to call if inconvenient
3 Courteous close

■ Request, for credit

If a buyer intends to make regular purchases from the same supplier it would be quite inconvenient to pay cash for each transaction separately. To avoid this, the buyer will ask for 'open account' terms so that purchases will be paid for monthly or quarterly.

Supplier requests open account terms

Dear

1 As you know we have placed many orders with you over the last 12 months and we have always been pleased with your services and products. As our business is growing we expect to place larger orders with you in the future.

2 I would be pleased if you could grant us open account terms with, say, quarterly settlements. This arrangement would avoid the inconvenience of our making separate payments on individual invoices.

3 Bankers' and trade references can be supplied on request.

4 I hope to hear from you soon.

Yours sincerely

1 Background information
2 Courteously request credit
3 Offer references
4 Close

R

Reply from buyer proposing alternative terms

Dear Mrs Adams

1 Thank you for your letter of 17 March asking for your business with us to be transferred to open account terms. We are pleased to hear that you have been satisfied with our services and products in the past.

2 Our business relations with you over the past 12 months have always been satisfactory, so we are happy to make this transfer, but based on a 60-day settlement period. It will not be necessary to supply references.

3 It is good to know that your business is expanding and we wish you well in the future.

Yours sincerely

1 Refer to letter
2 Courteously suggest alternative terms
3 Courteous close

■ Reservation

When you have visited a hotel to discuss reservation of its facilities for a function, it is usual to follow up with a letter as soon as possible and confirm what was discussed or agreed.

Confirmation of reservation

Dear Hilary

1 Thank you for your hospitality yesterday when I visited the Regent Prince Hotel. I was most impressed by your new banqueting facilities.

2 I confirm that I would like to reserve the Jasmine Suite for the retirement celebration of one of our senior directors. This will be held on Friday 14 August 2000 from 1830 to 2300 and we expect approximately 70 people to be present.

As we discussed, we shall require:

3
- 8 circular tables each seating 8 people
- One oblong head table seating 10 people
- Small flower arrangements on each table (colour scheme: red/white)
- A podium with microphone on a small raised stage
- A VCR and screen for showing a video
- Disco and DJ (meeting to be set up to discuss music requirements)

4 Thank you for giving me a selection of your menus. I have a meeting with the organising committee next week and will get back to you soon with our decision.

Yours sincerely

1 Refer to meeting
2 Confirm details – place, day, date, time, number of people
3 Use bullet points for details
4 Further details and close

■ Resignation

When you wish to leave your present company you will probably just hand in your notice, ie give your employer the required number of weeks' notice as stipulated in your letter of appointment or Contract of Employment. To do this formally you will write a letter of resignation.

Dear Mrs Long

1 I wish to give one month's notice of my resignation from the Company. My last day of work will be 31 October 200-.

2 I have been very happy working here for the past 3 years. My work was very challenging and enjoyable and I gained some valuable experience. However my husband has obtained a promotion which means we shall be moving to Glasgow, so of course this means a complete relocation for all the family.

3 Thank you for your help and guidance during my employment.

Yours sincerely

1 State period of notice and last day of work
2 Mention details of employment
3 Express thanks

R

■ Resumé

A resumé is often called a curriculum vitae, which is Latin and literally means 'the course of one's life'. It naturally follows, therefore, that this document should set out your personal details, education, qualifications and working experience. Make sure you organise all the information logically under headings and use columns where appropriate. All your details can then be found at a glance.

CURRICULUM VITAE

NAME	Jean Carson
ADDRESS	26 Gordon Road Chingford Essex CH4 6PY
TELEPHONE	0181 529 3456
DATE OF BIRTH	26 May 1965
NATIONALITY	British
MARITAL STATUS	Single

1

EDUCATION

2

1979 to 1983	Woodford High School
1983 to 1985	Bedford Business College (Business Course)

QUALIFICATIONS

3

GCE A Level	English Language Mathematics Spanish French
GCE O Level	Biology Philosophy Commerce History
LCCI	Private Secretary's Diploma
LCCI 3rd level	Text Production Audio Shorthand English for Business
RSA	140 wpm Shorthand
PITMAN	160 wpm Shorthand

SPECIAL AWARDS

4

RSA Silver medal for shorthand 140 wpm
Governors' prize for the first place in college examinations

1 Personal details should be shown at the beginning
2 State full and part time education courses
3 List qualifications in full (don't just say '4 A levels')
4 Mention any special achievements

5 **WORKING EXPERIENCE**

April 1988 to present	Personal Secretary to General Manager	Reliance Cables Vicarage Road Leyton LONDON E10 5RG
Sept 1985 to March 1988	Shorthand Typist	Bains, Hoyle & Co Solicitors 60 Kingsway LONDON WC2B 6AB

6 **INTERESTS**

Music; Languages; Hockey; Golf; Swimming

REFERENCES

7 1 Dr R G Davies
Principal
Bedford Secretarial College
Righton Road
Bedford MH2 2BS

2 Ms W Harris
Partner
Bains, Hoyle & Co
60 Kingsway
London WC2B 6AB

3 Mr W J Godfrey OBE
Managing Director
Reliance Cables
Vicarage Road
Leyton
London E10 5RG

8 June 2001

5 Mention your present job first and work backwards
6 Hobbies, interests or other relevant information
7 Give at least 2 referees – a former employer? a teacher?
8 Date your CV with month/year

R

S

■ Sales letter (see also CIRCULAR LETTER)

A sales letter aims to persuade readers that they need what you are trying to sell them and hopefully make them buy. Every sales letter must aim to meet the following general principles:

- **A**ttention — Attract the reader's attention – do this in the opening paragraph otherwise your letter will end up in the bin.
- **I**nterest — Create an interest by mentioning something which will appeal to readers. Encourage the reader to take notice of what you have to say.
- **D**esire — Arouse the reader's desire to buy, to attend a function to find out more or to contact the writer. Perhaps you can point out the benefits to readers and how they will affect them.
- **A**ction — Make the audience want to do something as a result of reading the ad. Maybe place an order, visit your showrooms, send back a reply form, arrange for a visit from your representative.

These AIDA principles are shown in these sample sales letters.

Sales appeal to efficiency

Dear Mr Wood

1 Reports from all over the world confirm what we have always known – that the RELIANCE solid tyre is the fulfilment of every car owner's dream.

2 You will naturally be well aware of the weaknesses of the ordinary air-filled tyre punctures, outer covers which split under sudden stress, and a tendency to skid on wet road surfaces, to mention only a few of motorist's main complaints. Our RELIANCE tyre enables you to offer your customers a tyre which is beyond criticism in those vital qualities of road-holding and reliability.

3 We could tell you a lot more about RELIANCE tyres but would prefer you to read the enclosed copies of reports from racing car drivers, test drivers, motor dealers and manufacturers. These reports really speak for themselves.

4 To encourage you to hold a stock of the new solid RELIANCE, we are pleased to offer you a special discount of 3% on any order received by 31 July.

Yours sincerely

S

1 Interest
2 Desire
3 Conviction
4 Action

Sales appeal to comfort

Dear Mrs Walker

1 What would you say to a gift that gave you a warmer and more comfortable home, free from draughts, and a saving of over 20% in fuel costs?

2 You can enjoy these advantages, not just this year but every year, simply by installing our SEALTITE panel system of double glazing. Can you think of a better gift for your entire family? The enclosed brochure will outline some of the benefits which make SEALTITE the most completely satisfactory double-glazing system on the market thanks to a number of features not provided in any other system.

3 Remember that the panels are precision-made by experienced craftsman to fit your own particular windows. Remember too that you will be dealing with a well established company which owes its success to the satisfaction given to scores of thousands of customers.

4 There is no need for you to make up your mind right now. First why not let us give you a free demonstration in your own home without any obligation whatsoever? If you are looking for an investment with an annual average return of over 20%, then here is your opportunity. If you post the enclosed card to reach us by the end of August, we can complete the installation for you in good time before winter sets in.

1 Interest
2 Desire
3 Conviction
4 Action

Sales appeal to leisure

Dear Mrs Hudson

1 'Modern scientific invention is a curse to the human race and will one day destroy it', said one of my customers recently. Rather a rash statement, and quite untrue for there are modern inventions which, far from being a curse, are real blessings.

2 Our new AQUAMASTER washer is just one of them. It takes all the hard work out of the weekly wash and makes washing a pleasure. All you have to do is put your soiled clothes in, press a button and sit back while the machine does the work. It does everything – washing, rinsing and drying – and we feel it does it quicker and better than any washing machine on the market today.

3 Come along and see the AQUAMASTER at work in our showroom. A demonstration will take up only a few minutes of your time, but it may rid you of your dread of washing day and make life much more pleasant.

4 I hope you will accept this invitation and come along soon to see what this latest of domestic time-savers can do for you.

Yours sincerely

1 Interest
2 Desire
3 Conviction
4 Action

Sales appeal to comfort

> Dear Sir
>
> At half the actual cost you can now have SOLAR HEATING installed in your home.
>
> As part of our research and development scheme introduced two years ago we are about to make our selection of a number of properties throughout the country as 'Research Homes' – yours could be one of them.
>
> The information received from selected 'Research Homes' in the past two years has proved that SOLAR HEATING is successful even in the most northern parts of the United Kingdom. This information has also enabled us to modify and improve our designs, which we will continue to do.
>
> If your home is selected as one of the properties to be included in our research scheme, we will bear half the actual cost of installation.
>
> If you are interested in helping our research programme in return for a half-price solar heating system, please complete the enclosed form and return it by the end of May. Within three weeks we will inform you if your home has been selected for the scheme.
>
> Yours faithfully

■ Staff circular (see NEWSLETTER, ARTICLE)

■ Structure

Short, routine documents need little thought or preparation. However very often many documents need careful thought and planning. If you learn this simple 4-point plan you will soon be structuring your documents logically so that they are clear, precise and very reader-friendly.

• **Introduction** (Background/Basics)	Why are you writing? Refer to a previous letter, contact or document
• **Details** (Facts and Figures)	Give instructions and/or information Ask for information Provide all relevant details Separate into paragraphs for separate themes Ensure a logical flow
• **Response or Action**	Tell the recipient what action you expect or state action you will take Give a general conclusion
• **Close**	A simple relevant closing sentence

This 4-point plan for all your business documents is illustrated here.

Institute of Secretaries
Wilson House, West Street, London SW1 2AR
Telephone 0181 987 2432
Fax 0181 987 2556

LD/ST

12 May 19—

Mrs Lesley Nunn
15 Windsor Road
Manchester
M2 9GJ

Dear Lesley

19— SECRETARIES CONFERENCE, 8/9 October 200_

1 As a valued member of the Institute of Secretaries, I have pleasure in inviting you to attend our special conference to be held at the Clifton Hotel, London on Tuesday/Wednesday 8/9 October 200_

This intensive, practical conference for professional secretaries aims to:

2
- increase your managerial and office productivity
- improve your communication skills
- bring you up-to-date with the latest technology and techniques
- enable networking with other secretaries

The seminar is power-packed with a distinguished panel of professional speakers who will give expert advice on many useful topics. A programme is enclosed giving full details of this seminar which I know you will not want to miss.

3 If you would like to join us please complete the enclosed registration form and return it to me before 30 June with your fee of £50 per person.

4 I look forward to seeing you again at this exciting conference.

Yours sincerely

Louise Dunscombe

LOUISE DUNSCOMBE (Mrs)
Conference Secretary

Encs

1 Opening (give a brief introduction)
2 Details (separate paragraphs, flowing logically)
3 Conclusion (action expected from the recipient)
4 Close (a simple closing statement)

■ Survey letter

Survey letter enclosing feedback form

Dear Mrs Taylor

1 At Global Insurance we are dedicated to providing you with the finest service possible. I should be grateful if you would evaluate our recent contact with you and tell us what we did right as well as identify any areas where improvements are necessary.

2 If you have received surveys in the past, Mrs Taylor, then I want to thank you and encourage you to respond again. Your comments will be most valuable and your suggestions will be followed up.

3 I sincerely appreciate your help and time taken to complete this survey, and assure you that your comments will receive my personal attention. I genuinely want to ensure that Global Insurance provides you with the first class service which you deserve and should be able to expect.

Yours sincerely

1 Background information
2 Keep the letter personal and informal
3 Express thanks and give an assurance of attention

■ Sympathy letter (see CONDOLENCE)

■ Tear-off slip (see also FORM, REPLY FORM)

A tear-off slip is used when you need a reply from many people. As the name implies, a tear-off slip is a section at the bottom of a letter, memo or other document, separated from the main document by a row of dashes or dots and possibly an illustration of a small pair of scissors.

Tear-off slip at foot of a letter

10th ANNIVERSARY CELEBRATION

Omega International is celebrating its 10th year of providing quality communications equipment. Approximately 50 representatives from Omega clients are expected to attend a special 10th Anniversary Celebration on Friday 29 October 200_.

The directors have decided to invite all employees who have been with Omega for at least 5 years to attend this special function. I am pleased to extend to you an invitation to join us at Omega's 10th Anniversary Celebration. Cocktails and a buffet supper will be provided.

This special function will take place from 1800 to 2300 hours at The Mandarin Suite, Oriental Hotel, West Street, London.

Please let me know whether you will be attending by returning the tear-off portion before 31 August.

I hope you will be able to join us.

....

1 Please return to Mrs Judy Brown, Administration Manager, before 31 August.

2 I shall/shall not* be attending the 10th Anniversary Celebration on Friday 29 October.

Name ....

3 Designation/Department ....

Signature .... Date ....

4 * Please delete as applicable.

1 For use internally, just include name/title; the full address is not required
2 Keep it simple and precise
3 Use double spacing
4 Remember footnote where appropriate

When designing the tear-off portion remember the general rules for design of forms of any kind, ie use double spacing for sections to be completed, and allow enough space for completion of the relevant information.

■ Terminology (see also ABC OF GOOD BUSINESS WRITING, JARGON, LANGUAGE, TONE)

Old fashioned terminology has no place in modern business writing. Such terminology will not only give a bad impression of the writer but it could even lead to confusion. Your documents should use no more words than are necessary to convey a clear, accurate message.

Don't say:	Say this instead:
We are in receipt of your letter of 25th inst.	Thank you for your letter of 25 August.
We acknowledge receipt of your recent letter.	Thank you for your letter of 25 August.
Enclosed herewith you will find …	I enclose
Please find enclosed …	I enclose
Please be good enough to advise me …	Please let me know
… regarding the above-mentioned	regarding this matter regarding this order

■ Testimonial (see also REFERENCE)

A testimonial is a letter of recommendation given by previous employers. They state the duration of employment, post(s) held, duties carried out, and also work attitude and personal qualities. The employee normally keeps the original testimonial and may send out a copy when applying for new jobs.

Testimonial

1 TO WHOM IT MAY CONCERN

2 Rachel Stewart was employed as Lecturer in Secretarial and Business Studies from March 1997 to June 1999.

3 During her employment Rachel taught Business Administration, Audio Transcription, Word Processing and Information Technology to students of a wide range of age and ability. She was Course Tutor for the full-time Business Administration Diploma students.

4 Rachel was a very dedicated teacher who always prepared for her classes thoroughly. She had a very organised approach to her duties especially the administrative responsibilities which she took on as Course Tutor. She also helped with programme marketing, curriculum planning and materials development in the department.

5 A very popular teacher, Rachel mixed very well with students and colleagues alike. She was a good time-keeper and enjoyed good health.

6 I am confident that Rachel will be a valuable asset to any organisation and can recommend her highly.

7

THOMAS LEONG
Head of Department - Business Studies

1 No formal addressee or salutation
2 State name, title and period of employment
3 Mention duties performed
4 Details of working attitude
5 Other personal details
6 A recommendation
7 No complimentary close

■ Thank you letter (see also REFUSAL)

When opening the day's mail it is always nice to find a thank you letter among the complaints and the bills. Take the opportunity to write thank you letters after a special lunch, a presentation, as an acknowledgement of good work. They only need to be brief and simple but you must ensure that they are warm and sincere.

Thank you for a Christmas present

> Dear William
>
> [1] I was delighted to receive your Christmas good cheer this morning – it was a very kind gesture. I will enjoy it over the festive season I'm sure.
>
> [2] Best wishes to you and your family for a very Happy Christmas and a prosperous New Year for your business.
>
> Yours sincerely

1 Keep it informal
2 Express good wishes

Thank you for a special lunch

> Dear Amelia
>
> [1] It was good to see you again yesterday and to discuss progress with my new book, *Pocket Business Communicator*. I was really pleased that you were able to bring along some page mock-ups and am particularly pleased with the concept you are proposing for the cover.
>
> [2] Special thanks for the lovely lunch at Pete's Place. The food and the hospitality there were particularly impressive. I shall look forward to a return visit in a couple of months when we meet again.
>
> Yours sincerely

1 Background details
2 Keep it informal

Thank you after training seminar

> Dear Mr Young
>
> [1] I enclose copies of the evaluation forms completed by our employees who attended your one day seminar last week. As you will see the response was excellent.
>
> [2] It has been a pleasure working with you on this project. I particularly appreciate how you tailored the seminar to meet our specific requirements.
>
> [3] I shall be in touch with you again as soon as we know our future training requirements.
>
> Yours sincerely

1 Enclose evaluation forms – state general consensus
2 Personal comments
3 Future contact

■ Tone (see also ABC OF GOOD BUSINESS WRITING, LANGUAGE, TERMINOLOGY)

If your message is to achieve its purpose the tone must be appropriate. If you use the wrong tone you could easily give the wrong impression or even upset and annoy the recipient.

Memos are usually written in a fairly informal style as you usually know the recipients fairly well. The major consideration will be the status of the sender and recipient in the organisation, and of course the topic of the memo. Try to adopt a tone which reflects these factors. When writing memos, avoid being impolite or abrupt (add 'Please …'); avoid over-politeness (do not say 'I should be very grateful …') and avoid unnecessary expressions (do not say 'Thank you' or 'Kind regards').

In letters your tone will also be dependent on your relationship with the recipient, the nature of the communication and the degree of importance or formality of the message. Take a look at these examples of different ways things can be written, and consider the reaction each would have if you were on the receiving end.

- *We cannot do anything about your problem.*
  Unfortunately we are unable to help you on this occasion.
- *This problem would not have happened if you had connected the wires properly.*
  The problem may be resolved by connecting the wires according to the instructions on page 2 of the manual.

- *Your television's guarantee has expired so you will have to pay for any repairs.*
  Unfortunately the guarantee for your television has expired. You will therefore be responsible for the cost of any repairs.
- *I am writing to complain because I am most unhappy with the way I was treated in your store today.*
  I am sorry to report that the standard of service I received in your store today was far below my expectations.

■ Trade reference

A trade reference is provided by a new buyer when he places an order with a new supplier. The reference will be the name of persons or companies to whom the supplier may refer for information about the buyer's business dealings.

Favourable reference

Dear Mr Newman

[1] Thank you for your letter of 29 July regarding Turner Printers. This company is a small but well-known and highly respectable firm which has been established in this town for more than 20 years.

[2] We have done business with Turner Printers for over 5 years on 90 day account terms, and they have always paid their account promptly on the due dates. We have allowed the company credit up to £10,000.

[3] I trust this information will be helpful to you.

Yours sincerely

1 Refer to letter
2 State relevant information and facts
3 Close

Reference suggesting caution

Dear Mr Wilson

1 Thank you for your letter of 29 July regarding Turner Printers.

This company has placed regular orders with us for about 5 years. Their account
2 with us is on 90 day terms. Although our business dealings have always been
satisfactory, unfortunately their accounts have not always been settled by the
due date. For this reason we have never allowed credit to reach the sum
3 mentioned in your letter. I believe this seems to be a case where caution is
necessary.

4 I hope this information will be treated as strictly confidential.

Yours sincerely

1 Refer to letter
2 State relevant information and facts
3 Suggest caution
4 Close

U

■ **Unwelcome news** (see CONDOLENCE, REDUNDANCY)

■ Voluntary offers (see also CIRCULAR LETTER, DONATION APPEAL, SALES LETTER and SURVEY LETTER)

A voluntary offer is one which is not asked for and which is sent to an individual or group of people. It serves the same purpose as a sales letter and follows the same general principles. A voluntary offer could be sent offering recipients free samples, goods on approval, special discounts, brochures/catalogues/price lists etc.

Offer of a demonstration

Dear Mrs Thornton

1 The Ideal Home Exhibition opens at Earls Court on Monday 21 June and you are certain to find attractive new designs in furniture as well as many new ideas.

2 The exhibition has much to offer which you will find useful, but we would like to extend our special invitation to our own display on Stand 26 where we shall be revealing our new WINDSOR range of unit furniture.

3 WINDSOR represents an entirely new concept in luxury unit furniture at very modest prices and we hope you will not miss the opportunity to see it for yourself. The inbuilt charm of this range comes from the use of solid elm and beech, combined with expert craftsmanship to give a perfect finish to each piece of furniture.

4 I enclose two admission tickets to the Ideal Home Exhibition. I am sure you will not want to miss this opportunity to see the variety of ways in which WINDSOR unit furniture can be arranged to suit any requirements.

I look forward to seeing you there.

Yours sincerely

1 What? Where? When?
2 Give further details
3 Encourage readers; create interest
4 Response required

Offer to new home owners

Dear Newcomers

1 Welcome to your new home! We have no wish to disturb you as you settle in but we would like to tell you why people in this town and the surrounding areas are very familiar with the name BAXENDALE.

2 Our store is situated at the corner of Grafton Street and Dorset Road and we invite you to visit us to see for yourself the exciting range of goods which have made us a household name.

3 Our well-known shopping guide is enclosed for you to browse through at your leisure. You will see practically everything you need to add to the comfort and beauty of your home.

4 As a special attraction to newcomers to the area we are offering a free gift worth £2 for every £20 spent in our store. The enclosed card is valid for one calendar month and it will entitle you to select goods of your own choice as your free gift.

We sincerely hope that you enjoy living in your new home.

Yours faithfully

1 Attention
2 Interest
3 Desire
4 Action

■ Warning letter (see also DISMISSAL)

A warning letter is sent to an employee whose work is unsatisfactory. As a general rule an employee must have received a warning before he or she may be dismissed. The company's rules regarding warnings and dismissal should be laid down in the Conditions of Employment or in the Employment Contract.

A warning letter will usually follow a face-to-face meeting when the employee's unsatisfactory work or attitude is discussed.

A warning for dishonesty

Dear John

1 Further to our meeting today I regret to confirm that I find your recent conduct totally unsatisfactory.

2 On 15 August a customer complained about your rudeness; then on 25 August you were found smoking in a prohibited area. On both occasions you were given a verbal warning from your supervisor.

3 If there is a repeat of any of these incidents, or any other breach of the company's standard codes of conduct, I shall view the situation very seriously.

4 I confirm that I will speak to you again in one month's time when your work attitude and performance will be reviewed.

Yours sincerely

1 Refer to meeting
2 Give specific details
3 State consequences of repeat
4 Confirm follow-up

A warning for lateness

Dear Andrew

1 You arrived at work at 9.40 am yesterday, the fourth day this month on which you have been late for work without giving any prior notice. This lateness has caused a great deal of inconvenience and disruption both to your supervisor and your colleagues.

2 Your terms of employment require you to work from 9 am to 5.30 pm. As you know, these working hours can only be varied by permission from your supervisor or head of department. In the circumstances I am forced to issue this official warning.

3 If you are late again without prior arrangement, the situation will be viewed very seriously and steps could be taken which could lead to your dismissal. I do hope that this will not be necessary and that you will make a serious effort to arrive at work on time.

4 This warning will remain in force for 6 months. If there are no further incidences of lateness within that period, it will then be deleted from your records.

Yours sincerely

1 Give specific details of lateness
2 Mention terms of employment
3 State consequences of continued lateness
4 Confirm period of warning

■ Writing style (see ABC OF GOOD BUSINESS WRITING, JARGON, LANGUAGE, TERMINOLOGY, TONE)